What Has Government Done to Our Money?

What Has Government Done to Our Money?

Murray N. Rothbard

MisesInstitute
Auburn, Alabama

Copyright © 1991, 2005, 2008 Ludwig von Mises Institute
Copyright © 1963, 1985, 1990 by Murray N. Rothbard
Copyright © 2005 Ludwig von Mises Institute, fifth edition

Published 2015 by the Mises Institute. This work is licensed under a Creative Commons Attribution-NonCommercial-NoDerivs 4.0 International License.
http://creativecommons.org/license/by-nc-nd/4.0/

Mises Institute
518 West Magnolia Avenue
Auburn, Alabama 36832
mises.org

ISBN: 978-1-61016-142-8 (paperback edition)
ISBN: 978-1-61016-645-4 (large format edition)

Contents

I.
Introduction

Few economic subjects are more tangled, more confused than money. Wrangles abound over "tight money" vs. "easy money," over the roles of the Federal Reserve System and the Treasury, over various versions of the gold standard, etc. Should the government pump money into the economy or siphon it out? Which branch of the government? Should it encourage credit or restrain it? Should it return to the gold standard? If so, at what rate? These and countless other questions multiply, seemingly without end.

Perhaps the Babel of views on the money question stems from man's propensity to be "realistic," i.e., to study only immediate political and economic problems. If we immerse ourselves wholly in day-to-day affairs, we cease making fundamental distinctions, or asking the really basic questions. Soon, basic issues are forgotten, and aimless drift is substituted for firm adherence to principle. Often we need to gain perspective, to stand aside from our everyday affairs in order to understand them more fully. This is particularly true in our economy, where interrelations are so intricate that we must isolate a few important factors, analyze them, and then trace their operations in the complex world. This was the point of "Crusoe economics," a favorite device of classical economic theory. Analysis of Crusoe and Friday on a desert island, much abused by critics as irrelevant to today's world, actually performed the very useful function of spotlighting the basic axioms of human action.

Of all the economic problems, money is possibly the most tangled, and perhaps where we most need perspective. Money, moreover, is the economic area most encrusted and entangled with centuries of government meddling. Many people—many economists—usually devoted to the free market stop short at money. Money, they insist, is different; it must be supplied by government and regulated by government. They never think of state control of money as interference in the free market; a free market in money is unthinkable to them. Governments must mint coins, issue paper, define "legal tender," create central banks, pump money in and out, "stabilize the price level," etc.

Historically, money was one of the first things controlled by government, and the free market "revolution" of the eighteenth and nineteenth centuries made very little dent in the monetary sphere. So it is high time that we turn fundamental attention to the life-blood of our economy—money.

Let us first ask ourselves the question: *Can* money be organized under the freedom principle? Can we have a free market in money as well as in other goods and services? What would be the shape of such a market? And what are the effects of various governmental controls? If we favor the free market in other directions, if we wish to eliminate government invasion of person and property, we have no more important task than to explore the ways and means of a free market in money.

II.
Money in a Free Society

1.
The Value of Exchange

How did money begin? Clearly, Robinson Crusoe had no need for money. He could not have eaten gold coins. Neither would Crusoe and Friday, perhaps exchanging fish for lumber, need to bother about money. But when society expands beyond a few families, the stage is already set for the emergence of money.

To explain the role of money, we must go even further back, and ask: why do men exchange at all? Exchange is the prime basis of our economic life. Without exchanges, there would be no real economy and, practically, no society. Clearly, a voluntary exchange occurs because both parties expect to benefit. An exchange is an agreement between A and B to transfer the goods or services of one man for the goods and services of the other. Obviously, both benefit because each values what he receives in exchange more than what he gives up. When Crusoe, say, exchanges some fish for lumber, he values the lumber he "buys" more than the fish he "sells," while Friday, on the contrary, values the fish more than the lumber. From Aristotle to Marx, men have mistakenly believed that an exchange records some sort of equality of value—that if one barrel of fish is exchanged for ten logs, there is some sort of underlying *equality* between them. Actually, the exchange was made only because each party valued the two products in *different* order.

Why should exchange be so universal among mankind? Fundamentally, because of the great *variety* in nature: the variety in man, and the diversity of location of natural resources. Every man has a different set of skills and aptitudes, and every plot of ground has its own unique features, its own distinctive resources. From this external natural fact of variety come exchanges; wheat in Kansas for iron in Minnesota; one man's medical services for another's playing of the violin. Specialization permits each man to develop his best skill, and allows each region to develop its own particular resources. If no one could exchange, if every man were forced to be completely self-sufficient, it is obvious that most of us would starve to death, and the rest would barely remain alive. Exchange is the lifeblood, not only of our economy, but of civilization itself.

2.
Barter

Yet, *direct exchange* of useful goods and services would barely suffice to keep an economy going above the primitive level. Such direct exchange—or *barter*—is hardly better than pure self-sufficiency. Why is this? For one thing, it is clear that very little production could be carried on. If Jones hires some laborers to build a house, with what will he pay them? With parts of the house, or with building materials they could not use? The two basic problems are "indivisibility" and "lack of coincidence of wants." Thus, if Smith has a plow, which he would like to exchange for several different things—say, eggs, bread, and a suit of clothes—how can he do so? How can he break up the plow and give part of it to a farmer and another part to a tailor? Even where the goods are divisible, it is generally impossible for two exchangers to find each other at the same time. If *A* has a supply of eggs for sale, and *B* has a pair of shoes, how can they get together if *A* wants a suit? And think of the plight of an economics teacher who has to find an egg-producer who wants to purchase a few economics lessons in return for his eggs! Clearly, any sort of civilized economy is impossible under direct exchange.

3. Indirect Exchange

But man discovered, in the process of trial and error, the route that permits a greatly-expanding economy: *indirect* exchange. Under indirect exchange, you sell your product not for a good which you need directly, but for another good which you then, in turn, sell for the good you want. At first glance, this seems like a clumsy and round-about operation. But it is actually the marvelous instrument that permits civilization to develop.

Consider the case of *A,* the farmer, who wants to buy the shoes made by *B*. Since *B* doesn't want his eggs, he finds what *B does* want—let's say butter. A then exchanges his eggs for C's butter, and sells the butter to *B* for shoes. He first buys the butter not because he wants it directly, but because it will permit him to get his shoes. Similarly, Smith, a plow-owner, will sell his plow for one commodity which he can more readily divide and sell—say, butter—and will then exchange parts of the butter for eggs, bread, clothes, etc. In both cases, the superiority of butter—the reason there is extra demand for it beyond simple consumption—is its greater *marketability.* If one good is more marketable than another—if everyone is confident that it will be more readily sold—then it will come into greater demand because it will be used as a *medium of exchange.* It will be the medium through which one specialist can exchange his product for the goods of other specialists.

Now just as in nature there is a great variety of skills and resources, so there is a variety in the marketability of goods. Some goods are more widely demanded than others, some are more divisible into smaller units without loss of value, some more durable over long periods of time, some more transportable over large distances. All of these advantages make for greater marketability. It is clear that in every society, the most marketable goods will be gradually selected as the media for exchange. As they are more and more selected as media, the demand for them increases because of this use, and so they become even more *marketable*. The result is a reinforcing spiral: more marketability causes wider use as a medium which causes more marketability, etc. Eventually, one or two commodities are used as general *media*—in almost all exchanges—and these are called money.

Historically, many different goods have been used as media: tobacco in colonial Virginia, sugar in the West Indies, salt in Abyssinia, cattle in ancient Greece, nails in Scotland, copper in ancient Egypt, and grain, beads, tea, cowrie shells, and fishhooks. Through the centuries, two commodities, *gold* and *silver,* have emerged as money in the free competition of the market, and have displaced the other commodities. Both are uniquely marketable, are in great demand as ornaments, and excel in the other necessary qualities. In recent times, silver, being relatively more abundant than gold, has been found more useful for smaller exchanges, while gold is more useful for larger transactions. At any rate, the important thing is that whatever the reason, the free market has found gold and silver to be the most efficient moneys.

This process: the cumulative development of a medium of exchange on the free market—is the only way money can become established. Money cannot originate in any other way, neither by everyone suddenly deciding to create money out of useless material, nor by government calling bits of paper "money." For embedded in the demand for money is knowledge of the money-prices of the immediate past; in contrast to directly-used consumers' or producers' goods, money must have preexisting prices on which to ground a demand. But the only way this can happen is by beginning with a useful commodity under barter, and then adding demand for a medium for exchange to the previous demand for direct use (e.g., for ornaments, in the case of gold).[1] Thus, government is powerless to create money for the economy; it can only be developed by the processes of the free market.

A most important truth about money now emerges from our discussion: money is a commodity. Learning this simple lesson is one of the world's most important tasks. So often have people talked about money as something much more or less than this. Money is not an abstract unit of account, divorceable from a concrete good; it is not a useless token only good for exchanging; it is not a "claim on society"; it is not a guarantee of a fixed price level. It is simply a commodity. It differs from other commodities in being demanded mainly as a medium of exchange. But aside from this, it is a commodity—and, like all commodities, it has an existing stock, it faces demands by people to buy and hold it, etc. Like all

---

[1] On the origin of money, cf. Carl Menger, *Principles of Economics* (Glencoe, Ill.: Free Press, 1950), pp. 257–71; Ludwig von Mises, *The Theory of Money and Credit,* 3rd ed. (New Haven, Conn.: Yale University Press, 1951), pp. 97–123.

commodities, its "price"—in terms of other goods—is determined by the interaction of its total supply, or stock, and the total demand by people to buy and hold it. (People "buy" money by selling their goods and services for it, just as they "sell" money when they buy goods and services.)

4. Benefits of Money

The emergence of money was a great boon to the human race. Without money—without a general medium of exchange—there could be no real specialization, no advancement of the economy above a bare, primitive level. With money, the problems of indivisibility and "coincidence of wants" that plagued the barter society all vanish. Now, Jones can hire laborers and pay them in . . . money. Smith can sell his plow in exchange for units of . . . money. The money-commodity is divisible into small units, and it is generally acceptable by all. And so all goods and services are sold for money, and then money is used to buy other goods and services that people desire. Because of money, an elaborate "structure of production" can be formed, with land, labor services, and capital goods cooperating to advance production at each stage and receiving payment in money.

The establishment of money conveys another great benefit. Since all exchanges are made in money, all the exchange-ratios are expressed in money, and so people can now compare the market worth of each good to that of every other good. If a TV set exchanges for three ounces of gold, and an automobile exchanges for sixty ounces of gold, then everyone can see that one automobile is "worth" twenty TV sets on the market. These exchange-ratios are *prices,* and the money-commodity serves as a common denominator for all prices. Only the establishment of money-prices on the market allows the development of a civilized economy, for only they permit businessmen to *calculate* economically. Businessmen can now judge how well they are satisfying consumer demands by seeing how the selling-prices of their products compare with the prices they have to pay productive factors (their "costs"). Since all these prices are expressed in terms of money, the businessmen can determine whether they are making profits or losses. Such calculations guide businessmen, laborers, and landowners in their search for monetary income on the market. Only such calculations can allocate resources to their most productive uses—to those uses that will most satisfy the demands of consumers.

Many textbooks say that money has several functions: a medium of exchange, unit of account, or "measure of values," a "store of value," etc. But it should be clear that all of these functions are simply corollaries of the one great function: the medium of exchange. Because gold is a general medium, it is most marketable, it can be stored to serve as a medium in the future as well as the present, and all prices are expressed in its terms.[2] Because gold is a commodity medium for all exchanges, it can serve as a unit of account for present, and expected future, prices. It is important to realize that money cannot be an abstract unit of account or claim, except insofar as it serves as a medium of exchange.

5. The Monetary Unit

Now that we have seen how money emerged, and what it does, we may ask: how is the money-commodity used? Specifically, what is the stock, or supply, of money in society, and how is it exchanged?

In the first place, most tangible physical goods are traded in terms of weight. Weight is the distinctive unit of a tangible commodity, and so trading takes place in terms of units like tons, pounds, ounces, grains, grams, etc.[3] Gold is no exception. Gold, like other commodities, will be traded in units of weight.[4]

It is obvious that the size of the common unit chosen in trading makes no difference to the economist. One country, on the metric system, may prefer to figure

---

[2] Money does not "measure" prices or values; it is the common denominator for their expression. In short, prices are expressed in money; they are not measured by it.

[3] Even those goods nominally exchanging in terms of *volume* (bale, bushel, etc.) tacitly assume a standard weight per unit volume.

[4] One of the cardinal virtues of gold as money is its *homogeneity*—unlike many other commodities, it has no differences in quality. An ounce of pure gold equals any other ounce of pure gold the world over.

in grams; England or America may prefer to reckon in grains or ounces. All units of weight are convertible into each other; one pound equals sixteen ounces; one ounce equals 437.5 grains or 28.35 grams, etc.

Assuming gold is chosen as the money, the size of the gold-unit used in reckoning is immaterial to us. Jones may sell a coat for one gold ounce in America, or for 28.35 grams in France; both prices are identical.

All this might seem like laboring the obvious, except that a great deal of misery in the world would have been avoided if people had fully realized these simple truths. Nearly everyone, for example, thinks of money as abstract units for something or other, each cleaving uniquely to a certain country. Even when countries were on the "gold standard," people thought in similar terms. American money was "dollars," French was "francs," German "marks," etc. All these were admittedly tied to gold, but all were considered sovereign and independent, and hence it was easy for countries to "go off the gold standard." *Yet all of these names were simply names for units of weight of gold or silver.*

The British "pound sterling" originally signified a pound weight of silver. And what of the dollar? The dollar began as the generally applied name of an ounce weight of silver coined by a Bohemian Count named Schlick, in the sixteenth century. The Count of Schlick lived in Joachim's Valley or Jaochimsthal. The Count's coins earned a great reputation for their uniformity and fineness, and they were widely called

"Joachim's thalers," or, finally, "thaler." The name "dollar" eventually emerged from "thaler."

On the free market, then, the various names that units may have are simply *definitions of units of weight.* When we were "on the gold standard" before 1933, people liked to say that the "price of gold" was "fixed at twenty dollars per ounce of gold." But this was a dangerously misleading way of looking at our money. Actually, "the dollar" was *defined* as the *name for* (approximately) 1/20 of an ounce of gold. It was therefore misleading to talk about "exchange rates" of one country's currency for another. The "pound sterling" did not really "exchange" for five "dollars."[5] The dollar was defined as 1/20 of a gold ounce, and the pound sterling was, at that time, defined as the name for 1/4 of a gold ounce, simply traded for 5/20 of a gold ounce. Clearly, such exchanges, and such a welter of names, were confusing and misleading. How they arose is shown below in the chapter on government meddling with money. In a purely free market, gold would simply be exchanged directly as "grams," grains, or ounces, and such confusing names as dollars, francs, etc., would be superfluous. Therefore, in this section, we will treat money as exchanging directly in terms of ounces or grams.

Clearly, the free market will choose as the common unit whatever size of the money-commodity is most

[5] Actually, the pound sterling exchanged for $4.87, but we are using $5 for greater convenience of calculation.

convenient. If platinum were the money, it would likely be traded in terms of fractions of an ounce; if iron were used, it would be reckoned in pounds or tons. Clearly, the size makes no difference to the economist.

6.
The Shape of Money

If the size or the name of the money-unit makes little economic difference; neither does the shape of the monetary metal. Since the commodity is the money, it follows that the *entire* stock of the metal, so long as it is available to man, constitutes the world's stock of money. It makes no real difference what shape any of the metal is at any time. If iron is the money, then *all* the iron is money, whether it is in the form of bars, chunks, or embodied in specialized machinery.[6] Gold has been traded as money in the raw form of nuggets, as gold dust in sacks, and even as jewelry. It should not be surprising that gold, or other moneys, can be traded in many forms, since their important feature is their weight.

It is true, however, that some shapes are often more convenient than others. In recent centuries, gold and silver have been broken down into *coins,* for smaller, day-to-day transactions, and into larger bars for bigger transactions. Other gold is transformed into jewelry and other ornaments. Now, any kind of transformation

[6] Iron hoes have been used extensively as money, both in Asia and Africa.

from one shape to another costs time, effort, and other resources. Doing this work will be a business like any other, and prices for this service will be set in the usual manner. Most people agree that it is legitimate for jewelers to make ornaments out of raw gold, but they often deny that the same applies to the manufacture of coins. Yet, on the free market, coinage is essentially a business like any other.

Many people believed, in the days of the gold standard, that coins were somehow more "really" money than plain, uncoined gold "bullion" (bars, ingots, or any other shape). It is true that coins commanded a premium over bullion, but this was not caused by any mysterious virtue in the coins; it stemmed from the fact that it cost more to manufacture coins from bullion than to remelt coins back into bullion. Because of this difference, coins were more valuable on the market.

7. Private Coinage

The idea of private coinage seems so strange today that it is worth examining carefully. We are used to thinking of coinage as a "necessity of sovereignty." Yet, after all, we are not wedded to a "royal prerogative," and it is the American concept that sovereignty rests, not in government, but in the people.

How would private coinage work? In the same way, we have said, as any other business. Each minter would produce whatever size or shape of coin is most pleasing to his customers. The price would be set by the free competition of the market.

The standard objection is that it would be too much trouble to weigh or assay bits of gold at every transaction. But what is there to prevent private minters from stamping the coin and guaranteeing its weight and fineness? Private minters can guarantee a coin at least as well as a government mint. Abraded bits of metal would not be accepted as coin. People would use the coins of those minters with the best reputation for good quality of product. We have seen that this is precisely how the "dollar" became prominent—as a competitive silver coin.

Opponents of private coinage charge that fraud would run rampant. Yet, these same opponents would trust government to provide the coinage. But if government is to be trusted at all, then surely, with private coinage, government could at least be trusted to prevent or punish fraud. It is usually assumed that the prevention or punishment of fraud, theft, or other crimes is the real justification for government. But if government cannot apprehend the criminal when private coinage is relied upon, what hope is there for a reliable coinage when the integrity of the private market place operators is discarded in favor of a government monopoly of coinage? If government cannot be trusted to ferret out the occasional villain in the free market in coin, why can government be trusted when it finds itself in a position of total control over money and may debase coin, counterfeit coin, or otherwise with full legal sanction perform as the sole villain in the market place? It is surely folly to say that government must socialize all property in order to prevent anyone from stealing property. Yet the reasoning behind abolition of private coinage is the same.

Moreover, all modern business is built on guarantees of standards. The drug store sells an eight ounce bottle of medicine; the meat packer sells a pound of beef. The buyer expects these guarantees to be accurate, and they are. And think of the thousands upon thousands of specialized, vital industrial products that must meet very narrow standards and specifications. The buyer of a ½ inch bolt must get a ½ inch bolt and not a mere ⅜ inch.

Yet, business has not broken down. Few people suggest that the government must nationalize the machine-tool industry as part of its job of defending standards against fraud. The modern market economy contains an infinite number of intricate exchanges, most depending on definite standards of quantity and quality. But fraud is at a minimum, and that minimum, at least in theory, may be prosecuted. So it would be if there were private coinage. We can be sure that a minter's customers, and his competitors, would be keenly alert to any possible fraud in the weight or fineness of his coins.[7]

---

[7] See Herbert Spencer, *Social Statics* (New York: D. Appleton 1890), p. 438.

Champions of the government's coinage monopoly have claimed that money is different from all other commodities, because "Gresham's Law" proves that "bad money drives out good" from circulation. Hence, the free market cannot be trusted to serve the public in supplying good money. But this formulation rests on a misinterpretation of Gresham's famous law. The law really says that "money overvalued artificially by government will drive out of circulation artificially undervalued money." Suppose, for example, there are one-ounce gold coins in circulation. After a few years of wear and tear, let us say that some coins weigh only .9 ounces. Obviously, on the free market, the worn coins would circulate at only 90 percent of the value of the full-bodied coins, and the nominal face-value of the former would have to be repudiated.[8] If anything, it will be the "bad" coins that will be driven from the market. But suppose the government decrees that everyone must treat the worn coins as equal to new, fresh coins, and must accept them equally in payment of debts. What has the government really done? It has imposed *price control* by coercion on the "exchange rate" between the two types of coin. By insisting on the par-ratio when the worn coins should exchange at 10 percent discount, it artificially *overvalues* the

[8] To meet the problem of wear-and-tear, private coiners might either set a time limit on their stamped guarantees of weight, or agree to recoin anew, either at the original or at the lower weight. We may note that in the free economy there will not be the compulsory standardization of coins that prevails when government monopolies direct the coinage.

worn coins and *undervalues* new coins. Consequently, everyone will circulate the worn coins, and hoard or export the new. "Bad money drives out good money," then, not on the free market, but as the direct result of governmental intervention in the market.

Despite never-ending harassment by governments, making conditions highly precarious, private coins have flourished many times in history. True to the virtual law that all innovations come from free individuals and not the state, the first coins were minted by private individuals and goldsmiths. In fact, when the government first began to monopolize the coinage, the royal coins bore the guarantees of private bankers, whom the public trusted far more, apparently, than they did the government. Privately-minted gold coins circulated in California as late as 1848.[9]

8.
The "Proper" Supply of Money

Now we may ask: what is the supply of money in society and how is that supply used? In particular, we may raise the perennial question, how much money

[9] For historical examples of private coinage, see B.W. Barnard, "The use of Private Tokens for Money in the United States," *Quarterly Journal of Economics* (1916–17): 617–26; Charles A. Conant, *The Principles of Money and Banking* (New York: Harper Bros., 1905), vol. I, pp. 127–32; Lysander Spooner, *A Letter to Grover Cleveland* (Boston: B.R. Tucker, 1886), p. 79; and J. Laurence Laughlin, *A New Exposition of Money, Credit and Prices* (Chicago: University of Chicago Press, 1931), vol. I, pp. 47–51. On coinage, also see Mises, *Theory of Money and Credit,* pp. 65–67; and Edwin Cannan, *Money,* 8th ed. (London: Staples Press, 1935), pp. 33ff.

"do we need"? Must the money supply be regulated by some sort of "criterion," or can it be left alone to the free market?

First, *the total stock, or supply, of money in society at any one time, is the total weight of the existing money-stuff.* Let us assume, for the time being, that only *one* commodity is established on the free market as money. Let us further assume that *gold* is that commodity (although we could have taken silver, or even iron; it is up to the *market,* and not to us, to decide the best commodity to use as money). Since money is gold, the total supply of money is the total weight of gold existing in society. The *shape* of gold does not matter—except if the cost of changing shapes in certain ways is greater than in others (e.g., minting coins costing more than melting them). In that case, one of the shapes will be chosen by the market as the money-of-account, and the other shapes will have a premium or discount in accordance with their relative costs on the market.

Changes in the total gold stock will be governed by the same causes as changes in other goods. Increases will stem from greater production from mines; decreases from being used up in wear and tear, in industry, etc. Because the market will choose a durable commodity as money, and because money is not used up at the rate of other commodities—but is employed as a medium of exchange—the proportion of new annual production to its total stock will tend to be quite small. Changes in total gold stock, then, generally take place very slowly.

What "should" the supply of money be? All sorts of criteria have been put forward: that money should move in accordance with population, with the "volume of trade," with the "amounts of goods produced," so as to keep the "price level" constant, etc. Few indeed have suggested leaving the decision to the market. But money differs from other commodities in one essential fact. And grasping this difference furnishes a key to understanding monetary matters. When the supply of any other good increases, this increase confers a social benefit; it is a matter for general rejoicing. More consumer goods mean a higher standard of living for the public; more capital goods mean sustained and increased living standards in the future. The discovery of new, fertile land or natural resources also promises to add to living standards, present and future. But what about money? Does an addition to the money supply also benefit the public at large?

Consumer goods are used up by consumers; capital goods and natural resources are used up in the process of producing consumer goods. But money is not used up; its function is to act as a medium of exchanges—to enable goods and services to travel more expeditiously from one person to another. These exchanges are all made in terms of money prices. Thus, if a television set exchanges for three gold ounces, we say that the "price" of the television set is three ounces. At any one time, all goods in the economy will exchange at certain gold-ratios or prices. As we have said, money, or gold, is the common denominator of all prices. But what of money itself? Does it have a "price"? Since a price is simply an exchange-ratio, it clearly does. But, in this case, the "price of money" is an *array* of the infinite number of exchange-ratios for all the various goods on the market.

Thus, suppose that a television set costs three gold ounces, an auto sixty ounces, a loaf of bread 1/100 of an ounce, and an hour of Mr. Jones's legal services one ounce. The "price of money" will then be an array of alternative exchanges. One ounce of gold will be "worth" either 1/3 of a television set, 1/60 of an auto, 100 loaves of bread, or one hour of Jones's legal service. And so on down the line. The price of money, then, is the "purchasing power" of the monetary unit—in this case, of the gold ounce. It tells what that ounce can purchase in exchange, just as the money-price of a television set tells how much money a television set can bring in exchange.

What determines the price of money? The same forces that determine all prices on the market—that venerable but eternally true law: "supply and demand." We all know that if the supply of eggs increases, the price will tend to fall; if the buyers' demand for eggs increases, the price will tend to rise. The same is true for money. An increase in the supply of money will tend to lower its "price;" an increase in the demand for money will raise it. But what is the demand for money? In the case of eggs, we know what "demand" means; it is the amount of money consumers are willing to spend on eggs, plus eggs retained and not sold by suppliers.

Similarly, in the case of money, "demand" means the various goods offered in exchange for money, plus the money retained in cash and not spent over a certain time period. In both cases, "supply" may refer to the total stock of the good on the market.

What happens, then, if the supply of gold increases, demand for money remaining the same? The "price of money" falls, i.e., the purchasing power of the money-unit will fall all along the line. An ounce of gold will now be worth less than 100 loaves of bread, ⅓ of a television set, etc. Conversely, if the supply of gold falls, the purchasing power of the gold-ounce rises.

What is the effect of a change in the money supply? Following the example of David Hume, one of the first economists, we may ask ourselves what would happen if, overnight, some good fairy slipped into pockets, purses, and bank vaults, and doubled our supply of money. In our example, she magically doubled our supply of gold. Would we be twice as rich? Obviously not. What makes us rich is an abundance of goods, and what limits that abundance is a scarcity of resources: namely land, labor, and capital. Multiplying coin will not whisk these resources into being. We may *feel* twice as rich for the moment, but clearly all we are doing is *diluting* the money supply. As the public rushes out to spend its new-found wealth, prices will, very roughly, double—or at least rise until the demand is satisfied, and money no longer bids against itself for the existing goods.

Thus, we see that while an increase in the money supply, like an increase in the supply of any good, lowers its price, the change *does not—unlike other goods—confer a social benefit.* The public at large is not made richer. Whereas new consumer or capital goods add to standards of living, new money only raises prices—i.e., dilutes its own purchasing power. The reason for this puzzle is that money is *only useful for its exchange value.* Other goods have various "real" utilities, so that an increase in their supply satisfies more consumer wants. Money has only utility for prospective exchange; its utility lies in its exchange value, or "purchasing power." Our law—that an increase in money does not confer a social benefit—stems from its unique use as a medium of exchange.

An increase in the money supply, then, only dilutes the effectiveness of each gold ounce; on the other hand, a fall in the supply of money raises the power of each gold ounce to do its work. We come to the startling truth that it *doesn't matter what the supply of money is.* Any supply will do as well as any other supply. The free market will simply adjust by changing the purchasing power, or effectiveness of the gold-unit. There is no need to tamper with the market in order to alter the money supply that it determines.

At this point, the monetary planner might object: "All right, granting that it is pointless to increase the money supply, isn't gold mining a waste of resources? Shouldn't the government keep the money supply constant, and prohibit new mining?" This argument might be plausible to those who hold no principled objections to government meddling, though it would not convince the determined advocate of liberty. But the objection overlooks an important point: that gold is not only money, but is also, inevitably, a *commodity*. An increased supply of gold may not confer any *monetary* benefit, but it does confer a *non-monetary* benefit—i.e., it does increase the supply of gold used in consumption (ornaments, dental work, and the like) and in production (industrial work). Gold mining, therefore, is not a social waste at all.

We conclude, therefore, that determining the supply of money, like all other goods, is best left to the free market. Aside from the general moral and economic advantages of freedom over coercion, no dictated quantity of money will do the work better, and the free market will set the production of gold in accordance with its relative ability to satisfy the needs of consumers, as compared with all other productive goods.[10]

9. The Problem of "Hoarding"

The critic of monetary freedom is not so easily silenced, however. There is, in particular, the ancient bugbear of "hoarding." The image is conjured up of the selfish old miser who, perhaps irrationally, perhaps from evil motives, hoards up gold unused in his cellar or treasure trove—thereby stopping the flow of

[10] Gold mining is, of course, no more profitable than any other business; in the long-run, its rate of return will be equal to the net rate of return in any other industry.

circulation and trade, causing depressions and other problems. Is hoarding really a menace?

In the first place, what has simply happened is an increased demand for money on the part of the miser. As a result, prices of goods fall, and the purchasing power of the gold-ounce rises. There has been no loss to society, which simply carries on with a lower active supply of more "powerful" gold ounces.

Even in the worst possible view of the matter, then, nothing has gone wrong, and monetary freedom creates no difficulties. But there is more to the problem than that. For it is by no means irrational for people to desire *more* or *less* money in their cash balances.

Let us, at this point, study cash balances further. Why do people keep any cash balances at all? Suppose that all of us were able to foretell the future with absolute certainty. In that case, no one would have to keep cash balances on hand. Everyone would know exactly how much he will spend, and how much income he will receive, at all future dates. He need not keep any money at hand, but will lend out his gold so as to receive his payments in the needed amounts on the very days he makes his expenditures. But, of course, we necessarily live in a world of *uncertainty*. People do not precisely know what will happen to them, or what their future incomes or costs will be. The more uncertain and fearful they are, the more cash balances they will want to hold; the more secure, the less cash they will wish to keep on hand. Another reason for keeping cash is also a function of the real world of uncertainty.

If people expect the price of money to fall in the near future, they will spend their money now while money is more valuable, thus "dishoarding" and reducing their demand for money. Conversely, if they expect the price of money to rise, they will wait to spend money later when it is more valuable, and their demand for cash will increase. People's demands for cash balances, then, rise and fall for good and sound reasons.

Economists err if they believe something is wrong when money is not in constant, active "circulation." Money is only useful for exchange value, true, *but it is not only useful at the actual moment of exchange.* This truth has been often overlooked. Money is just as useful when lying "idle" in somebody's cash balance, even in a miser's "hoard."[11] For that money is being held now in wait for possible future exchange—it supplies to its owner, right now, the usefulness of permitting exchanges at any time—present or future—the owner might desire.

It should be remembered that all gold must be owned by someone, and therefore that all gold must be held in people's cash balances. If there are 3,000 tons of gold in the society, all 3,000 tons must be owned and held, at any one time, in the cash balances of individual people. The total sum of cash balances is always identical with the total supply of money

[11] At what point does a man's cash balance become a faintly disreputable "hoard," or the prudent man a miser? It is impossible to fix any definite criterion: generally, the charge of "hoarding" means that *A* is keeping more cash than *B* thinks is appropriate for *A*.

in the society. Thus, ironically, if it were not for the uncertainty of the real world, there could be no monetary system at all! In a certain world, no one would be willing to hold cash, so the demand for money in society would fall infinitely, prices would skyrocket without end, and any monetary system would break down. Instead of the existence of cash balances being an annoying and troublesome factor, interfering with monetary exchange, it is absolutely necessary to any monetary economy.

It is misleading, furthermore, to say that money "circulates." Like all metaphors taken from the physical sciences, it connotes some sort of mechanical process, independent of human will, which moves at a certain speed of flow, or "velocity." Actually, money does not "circulate"; it is, from time, to time, *transferred* from one person's cash balance to another's. The existence of money, once again, depends upon people's willingness to hold cash balances.

At the beginning of this section, we saw that "hoarding" never brings any loss to society. Now, we will see that movement in the price of money caused by changes in the demand for money yields a positive social benefit—as positive as any conferred by increased supplies of goods and services. We have seen that the total sum of cash balances in society is equal and identical with the total supply of money. Let us assume the supply remains constant, say at 3,000 tons. Now, suppose, for whatever reason—perhaps growing apprehension—people's demand for cash balances increases. Surely, it is a positive social benefit to satisfy this demand. But how can it be satisfied when the total sum of cash must remain the same? Simply as follows: with people valuing cash balances more highly, the demand for money increases, and prices fall. As a result, the same total sum of cash balances now confers a higher "real" balance, i.e., it is higher in proportion to the prices of goods—to the work that money has to perform. In short, the effective cash balances of the public have increased. Conversely, a fall in the demand for cash will cause increased spending and higher prices. The public's desire for lower effective cash balances will be satisfied by the necessity for given total cash to perform more work.

Therefore, while a change in the price of money stemming from changes in supply merely alters the effectiveness of the money-unit and confers no social benefit, a fall or rise caused by a change in the *demand for* cash balances *does* yield a social benefit—for it satisfies a public desire for either a higher or lower proportion of cash balances to the work done by cash. On the other hand, an increased *supply* of money will *frustrate* public demand for a more *effective* sum total of cash (more effective in terms of purchasing power).

People will almost always say, if asked, that they want as much money as they can get! But what they really want is not more units of money—more gold ounces or "dollars"—but more *effective* units, i.e., greater command of goods and services bought by money. We have seen that society cannot satisfy its demand for more money by increasing its supply—for an increased supply will simply *dilute* the effectiveness of each ounce, and the money will be no more really plentiful than before. People's standard of living (except in the nonmonetary uses of gold) cannot increase by mining more gold. If people want more effective gold ounces in their cash balances, they can get them only through a fall in prices and a rise in the effectiveness of each ounce.

10.
Stabilize the Price Level?

Some theorists charge that a free monetary system would be unwise, because it would not "stabilize the price level," i.e., the price of the money-unit. Money, they say, is supposed to be a fixed yardstick that never changes. Therefore, its value, or purchasing power, should be stabilized. Since the price of money would admittedly fluctuate on the free market, freedom must be overruled by government management to insure stability.[12] Stability would provide justice, for example, to debtors and creditors, who will be sure of paying back dollars, or gold ounces, of the same purchasing power as they lent out.

Yet, if creditors and debtors want to hedge against future changes in purchasing power, they can do so

[12] How the government would go about this is unimportant at this point. Basically, it would involve governmentally-managed changes in the money supply.

easily on the free market. When they make their contracts, they can agree that repayment will be made in a sum of money *adjusted* by some agreed-upon index number of changes in the value of money. The stabilizers have long advocated such measures, but strangely enough, the very lenders and borrowers who are supposed to benefit most from stability, have rarely availed themselves of the opportunity. Must the government then force certain "benefits" on people who have already freely rejected them? Apparently, businessmen would rather take their chances, in this world of irremediable uncertainty, on their ability to anticipate the conditions of the market. After all, the price of money is no different from any other free price on the market. They can change in response to changes in demand of individuals; why not the monetary price?

Artificial stabilization would, in fact, seriously distort and hamper the workings of the market. As we have indicated, people would be unavoidably frustrated in their desires to alter their real proportion of cash balances; there would be no opportunity to change cash balances in proportion to prices. Furthermore, improved standards of living come to the public from the fruits of capital investment. Increased productivity tends to lower prices (and costs) and thereby distribute the fruits of free enterprise to all the public, raising the standard of living of all consumers. Forcible propping up of the price level prevents this spread of higher living standards.

Money, in short, is not a "fixed yardstick." It is a commodity serving as a medium for exchanges.

Flexibility in its value in response to consumer demands is just as important and just as beneficial as any other free pricing on the market.

11.
Coexisting Moneys

So far we have obtained the following picture of money in a purely free economy: gold or silver coming to be used as a medium of exchange; gold minted by competitive private firms, circulating by weight; prices fluctuating freely on the market in response to consumer demands and supplies of productive resources. Freedom of prices necessarily implies freedom of movement for the purchasing power of the money-unit; it would be impossible to use force and interfere with movements in the value of money without simultaneously crippling freedom of prices for all goods. The resulting free economy would not be chaotic. On the contrary, the economy would move swiftly and efficiently to supply the wants of consumers. The money market can also be free.

Thus far, we have simplified the problem by assuming only one monetary metal—say, gold. Suppose that *two* or more moneys continue to circulate on the world market—say, gold and silver. Possibly, gold will be the money in one area and silver in another, or else they both may circulate side by side. Gold, for example, being ounce-for-ounce more valuable on the market than silver, may be used for larger transactions and silver for smaller. Would not two moneys be impossibly chaotic? Wouldn't the government have to step in and impose a fixed ration between the two ("bimetallism") or in some way demonetize one or the other metal (impose a "single standard")?

It is very possible that the market, given free rein, might eventually establish one single metal as money. But in recent centuries, silver stubbornly remained to challenge gold. It is not necessary, however, for the government to step in and save the market from its own folly in maintaining two moneys. Silver remained in circulation precisely because it was convenient (for small change, for example). Silver and gold could easily circulate side by side, and have done so in the past. The relative supplies of and demands for the two metals will determine the exchange rate between the two, and this rate, *like any other price,* will continually fluctuate in response to these changing forces. At one time, for example, silver and gold ounces might exchange at 16:1, another time at 15:1, etc. Which metal will serve as a unit of account depends on the concrete circumstances of the market. If gold is the money of account, then most transactions will be reckoned in gold ounces, and silver ounces will exchange at a freely-fluctuating price in terms of the gold.

It should be clear that the exchange rate and the purchasing powers of the units of the two metals will always tend to be proportional. If prices of goods are fifteen times as much in silver as they are in gold, then the exchange rate will tend to be set at 15:1. If not, it will pay to exchange from one to the other until parity is reached. Thus, if prices are fifteen times as much in terms of silver as gold while silver/ gold is 20:1, people will rush to sell their goods for gold, buy silver, and then rebuy the goods with silver, reaping a handsome gain in the process. This will quickly restore the "purchasing power parity" of the exchange rate; as gold gets cheaper in terms of silver, silver prices of goods go up, and gold prices of goods go down.

The free market, in short, is eminently *orderly* not only when money is free but even when there is more than one money circulating.

What kind of "standard" will a free money provide? The important thing is that the standard not be imposed by government decree. If left to itself, the market may establish gold as a single money ("gold standard"), silver as a single money ("silver standard"), or, perhaps most likely, both as moneys with freely-fluctuating exchange rates ("parallel standards").[13]

---

[13] For historical examples of parallel standards, see W. Stanley Jevons, *Money and the Mechanism of Exchange* (London: Kegan Paul, 1905), pp. 88–96, and Robert S. Lopez, "Back to Gold, 1252," *Economic History Review* (December 1956): 224. Gold coinage was introduced into modern Europe almost simultaneously in Genoa and Florence. Florence instituted bimetallism, while "Genoa, on the contrary, in conformity to the principle of restricting state intervention as much as possible, did not try to enforce a fixed relation between coins of different metals," ibid. On the theory of parallel standards, see Mises, *Theory of Money and Credit,* pp. 179f. For a proposal that the United States go onto a parallel standard, by an official of the U.S. Assay Office, see I.W. Sylvester, *Bullion Certificates as Currency* (New York, 1882).

12.
Money Warehouses

Suppose, then, that the free market has established gold as money (forgetting again about silver for the sake of simplicity). Even in the convenient shape of coins, gold is often cumbersome and awkward to carry and use directly in exchange. For larger transactions, it is awkward and expensive to transport several hundred pounds of gold. But the free market, ever ready to satisfy social needs, comes to the rescue. Gold, in the first place, must be stored somewhere, and just as specialization is most efficient in other lines of business, so it will be most efficient in the warehousing business. Certain firms, then, will be successful on the market in providing warehousing services. Some will be gold warehouses, and will store gold for its myriad owners. As in the case of all warehouses, the owner's right to the stored goods is established by a *warehouse receipt* which he receives in exchange for storing the goods. The receipt entitles the owner to claim his goods at any time he desires. This warehouse will earn profit no differently from any other—i.e., by charging a price for its storage services.

There is every reason to believe that gold warehouses, or money warehouses, will flourish on the free market in the same way that other warehouses will prosper. In fact, warehousing plays an even more important role in the case of money. For all other goods pass into consumption, and so must leave the warehouse after a while to be used up in production or consumption. But money, as we have seen, is mainly not "used" in the physical sense; instead, it is used to exchange for other goods, and to lie in wait for such exchanges in the future. In short, money is not so much "used up" as simply transferred from one person to another.

In such a situation, convenience inevitably leads to *transfer of the warehouse receipt instead of the physical gold itself.* Suppose, for example, that Smith and Jones both store their gold in the same warehouse. Jones sells Smith an automobile for 100 gold ounces. They could go through the expensive process of Smith's redeeming his receipt, and moving their gold to Jones's office, with Jones turning right around and redepositing the gold again. But they will undoubtedly choose a far more convenient course: Smith simply gives Jones a warehouse receipt for 100 ounces of gold.

In this way, warehouse receipts for money come more and more to function as *money substitutes.* Fewer and fewer transactions move the actual gold; in more and more cases paper titles to the gold are used instead. As the market develops, there will be three limits on the advance of this substitution process. *One* is the extent that people us these money warehouses—called *banks*—instead of cash. Clearly, if Jones, for some reason, didn't like to use a bank, Smith would have to transport the actual gold. The *second* limit is the extent of the clientele of *each bank.* In other words, the more transactions taking place between clients of *different* banks, the more gold will have to be transported. The more exchanges are made by clients of the same bank, the less need to transport the gold. If Jones and Smith were clients of different warehouses, Smith's bank (or Smith himself) would have to transport the gold to Jones's bank. *Third,* the clientele must have confidence in the trustworthiness of their banks. If they suddenly find out, for example, that the bank officials have had criminal records, the bank will likely lose its business in short order. In this respect, all warehouses—and all businesses resting on good will—are alike.

As banks grow and confidence in them develops, their clients may find it more convenient in many cases to waive their right to paper receipts—called *bank notes—and, instead, to keep their titles as open book accounts.* In the monetary realm, these have been called *bank deposits.* Instead of transferring paper receipts, the client has a book claim at the bank; he makes exchanges by writing an order to his warehouse to transfer a portion of this account to someone else. Thus, in our example, Smith will order the bank to transfer book title to his 100 gold ounces to Jones. This written order is called a *check.*

It should be clear that, economically, there is no difference whatever between a bank note and a bank deposit. Both are claims to ownership of stored gold; both are transferred similarly as money substitutes, and both have the identical three limits on their extent of use. The client can choose, according to this convenience, whether he wishes to keep his title in note, or deposit, form.[14]

Now, what has happened to their money supply as a result of all these operations? If paper notes or bank deposits are used as "money substitutes," does this mean that the effective money supply in the economy has increased even though the stock of gold has remained the same? Certainly not. For the money substitutes are simply warehouse receipts for actually-deposited gold. If Jones deposits 100 ounces of gold in his warehouse and gets a receipt for it, the receipt can be used on the market as money, but only as a convenient *stand-in* for the gold, not as an increment. The gold in the vault is then no longer a part of the effective money supply, but is held as a *reserve* for its receipt, to be claimed whenever desired by its owner. An increase or decrease in the use of substitutes, then, exerts no change on the money supply. Only the *form* of the supply is changed, not the total. Thus the money supply of a community may begin as ten million gold ounces. Then, six million may be deposited in banks, in return for gold notes, whereupon the effective supply will now be: four million ounces of gold, six million ounces of gold claims in paper notes. The total money supply has remained the same.

Curiously, many people have argued that it would be impossible for banks to make money if they were to

[14] A third form of money-substitute will be *token coins* for very small change. These are, in effect, equivalent to bank notes, but "printed" on base metal rather than on paper.

operate on this "100 percent reserve" basis (gold always represented by its receipt). Yet, there is no real problem, any more than for any warehouse. Almost all warehouses keep all the goods for their owners (100 percent reserve) as a matter of course—in fact, it would be considered fraud or theft to do otherwise. Their profits are earned from service charges to their customers. The banks can charge for their services in the same way. If it is objected that customers will not pay the high service charges, this means that the banks' services are not in very great demand, and the use of their services will fall to the levels that consumers find worthwhile.

We come now to perhaps the thorniest problem facing the monetary economist: an evaluation of "fractional reserve banking." We must ask the question: would fractional reserve banking be permitted in a free market, or would it be proscribed as fraud? It is well-known that banks have rarely stayed on a "100 percent" basis very long. Since money can remain in the warehouse for a long period of time, the bank is tempted to use some of the money for its own account—tempted also because people do not ordinarily care whether the gold coins they receive back from the warehouse are the identical gold coins they deposited. The bank is tempted, then to use other people's money to earn a profit for itself.

If the banks lend out the gold directly, the receipts, of course, are now partially invalidated. There are now some receipts with no gold behind them; in short, the bank is effectively insolvent, since it cannot possibly meet its own obligations if called upon to do so. It cannot possibly hand over its customers' property, should they all so desire.

Generally, banks, instead of taking the gold directly, print uncovered or "pseudo" warehouse receipts, i.e., warehouse receipts for gold that is not and cannot be there. These are then loaned at a profit. Clearly, the economic effect is the same. More warehouse receipts are printed than gold exists in the vaults. What the bank has done is to issue gold warehouse receipts which represent nothing, but are supposed to represent 100 percent of their face value in gold. The pseudo-receipts pour forth on the trusting market in the same way as the true receipts, and thus add to the effective money supply of the country. In the above example, if the banks now issue two million ounces of false receipts, with no gold behind them, the money supply of the country will rise from ten to twelve million gold ounces—at least until the hocus-pocus has been discovered and corrected. There are now, in addition to four million ounces of gold held by the public, eight million ounces of money substitutes, only six million of which are covered by gold.

Issue of pseudo-receipts, like counterfeiting of coin, is an example of *inflation,* which will be studied further below. *Inflation* may be defined as *any increase in the economy's supply of money not consisting of an increase in the stock of the money metal.* Fractional reserve banks, therefore, are inherently inflationary institutions.

Defenders of banks reply as follows: the banks are simply functioning like other businesses—they take risks. Admittedly, if all the depositors presented their claims, the banks would be bankrupt, since outstanding receipts exceed gold in the vaults. But, banks simply take the chance—usually justified—that not everyone will ask for his gold. The great difference, however, between the "fractional reserve" bank and all other business is this: other businessmen use their own or borrowed capital in ventures, and if they borrow credit, they promise to pay at a future date, taking care to have enough money at hand on that date to meet their obligation. If Smith borrows 100 gold ounces for a year, he will arrange to have 100 gold ounces available on that future date. But the bank isn't borrowing from its depositors; it doesn't pledge to pay back gold at a certain date in the future. Instead, it pledges to pay the receipt in gold at any time, on demand. In short, the bank note or deposit is not an IOU, or debt; it is a warehouse receipt for other people's property. Further, when a businessman borrows or lends money, he does not add to the money supply. The loaned funds are *saved* funds, part of the existing money supply being transferred from saver to borrower. Bank issues, on the other hand, artificially increase the money supply since pseudo-receipts are injected into the market.

A bank, then, is not taking the usual business risk. It does not, like all businessmen, arrange the time pattern of its assets proportionately to the time pattern of liabilities, i.e., see to it that it will have enough money, on due dates, to pay its bills. Instead, most of its liabilities are instantaneous, but its assets are not.

The bank creates new money out of thin air, and does not, like everyone else, have to acquire money by producing and selling its services. In short, the bank is *already* and at all times bankrupt; but its bankruptcy is only *revealed* when customers get suspicious and precipitate "bank runs." No other business experiences a phenomenon like a "run." No other business can be plunged into bankruptcy overnight simply because its customers decide to repossess their own property. No other business creates fictitious new money, which will evaporate when truly gauged.

The dire economic effects of fractional bank money will be explored in the next chapter. Here we conclude that, morally, such banking would have no more right to exist in a truly free market than any other form of implicit theft. It is true that the note or deposit does not actually say on its face that the warehouse guarantees to keep a full backing of gold on hand at all times. But the bank does promise to redeem on demand, and so when it issues any fake receipts, it is already committing fraud, since it immediately becomes impossible for the bank to keep its pledge and redeem all of its notes and deposits.[15] Fraud, therefore, is immediately being committed when the act of issuing pseudo-receipts takes place. *Which* particular receipts are fraudulent

[15] See Amasa Walker, *The Science of Wealth,* 3rd ed. (Boston: Little, Brown, 1867), pp. 139–41; and pp. 126–232 for an excellent discussion of the problems of a fractional-reserve money.

can only be discovered *after* a run on the bank has occurred (since all the receipts look alike), and the late-coming claimants are left high and dry.[16]

If fraud is to be proscribed in a free society, then fractional reserve banking would have to meet the same fate.[17] Suppose, however, that fraud and fractional reserve banking are permitted, with the banks only required to fulfill their obligations to redeem in gold on demand. Any failure to do so would mean instant bankruptcy. Such a system has come to be known as "free banking." Would there then be a heavy fraudulent issue of money substitutes, with resulting artificial creation of new money? Many people have assumed so, and believed that "wildcat banking" would then simply inflate the money supply astronomically. But, on the contrary, "free banking" would lead to a far "harder" monetary system than we have today.

The banks would be checked by the same three limits that we noted above, and checked rather rigorously.

---

[16] Perhaps a libertarian system would consider "general warrant deposits" (which allow the warehouse to return any homogeneous good to the depositor) as "specific warrant deposits," which, like bills of lading, pawn tickets, dock warrants, etc., establish ownership to certain specific earmarked objects. For, in the case of a general deposit warrant, the warehouse is tempted to treat the goods as its *own* property, instead of being the property of its customers. This is precisely what the banks have been doing. See Jevons, *Money and the Medium of Exchange,* pp. 207–12.

[17] Fraud is *implicit* theft, since it means that a contract has not been completed after the value has been received. In short, if *A* sells *B* a box labeled "corn flakes" and it turns out to be straw upon opening, *A*'s fraud is really theft of *B*'s property. Similarly, the issue of warehouse receipts for nonexistent goods, identical with genuine receipts, is fraud upon those who possess claims to nonexistent property.

In the first place, each bank's expansion will be limited by a loss of gold to another bank. For a bank can only expand money within the limits of its *own* clientele. Suppose, for example, that Bank A, with 10,000 ounces of gold deposited, now issues 2,000 ounces of false warehouse receipts to gold, and lends them to various enterprises, or invests them in securities. The borrower, or former holder of securities, will spend the new money on various goods and services. Eventually, the money going the rounds will reach an owner who is a client of *another* bank, *B*.

At that point, Bank *B* will call upon Bank *A* to redeem its receipt in gold, so that the gold can be transferred to Bank *B*'s vaults. Clearly, the wider the extent of each bank's clientele, and the more the clients trade with one another, the more scope there is for each bank to expand its credit and money supply. For if the bank's clientele is narrow, then soon after its issue of created money, it will be called upon to redeem—and, as we have seen, it doesn't have the wherewithal to redeem more than a fraction of its obligations. To avoid the threat of bankruptcy from this quarter, then, the narrower the scope of a bank's clientele, the greater the fraction of gold it must keep in reserve, and the less it can expand. If there is one bank in each country, there will be far more scope for expansion than if there is one bank for every two persons in the community. Other things being equal, then, the more banks there are, and the tinier their size, the "harder"—and better—the monetary supply will be. Similarly, a bank's clientele will also be limited by those who don't use a bank at all. The more people use actual gold instead of bank money, the less room there is for bank inflation.

Suppose, however, that the banks form a cartel, and agree to pay out each other's receipts, and not call for redemption. And suppose further that bank money is in universal use. Are there any limits left on bank expansion? Yes, there remains the check of client confidence in the banks. As bank credit and the money supply expand further and further, more and more clients will get worried over the lowering of the reserve fraction. And, in a truly free society, those who know the truth about the real insolvency of the banking system will be able to form AntiBank Leagues to urge clients to get their money out before it is too late. In short, leagues to urge bank runs, or the threat of their formation, will be able to stop and reverse the monetary expansion.

None of this discussion is meant to impugn the general practice of *credit,* which has an important and vital function on the free market. In a credit transaction, the possessor of money (a good useful in the present) exchanges it for an IOU payable at some future date (the IOU being a "future good") and the interest charge reflects the higher valuation of present goods over future goods on the market. But bank notes or deposits are *not* credit; they are warehouse receipts, instantaneous claims to cash (e.g., gold) in the bank vaults. The debtor makes sure that he pays his debt when payment becomes due; the fractional reserve banker can never pay more than a small fraction of his outstanding liabilities.

We turn, in the next chapter, to a study of the various forms of governmental interference in the monetary system—most of them designed, not to repress fraudulent issue, but on the contrary, to remove these and other natural checks on inflation.

13.
Summary

What have we learned about money in a free society? We have learned that *all* money has originated, and must originate, in a useful commodity chosen by the free market as a medium of exchange. The unit of money is simply a unit of weight of the monetary commodity—usually a metal, such as gold or silver. Under freedom, the commodities chosen as money, their shape and form, are left to the voluntary decisions of free individuals. Private coinage, therefore, is just as legitimate and worthwhile as any business activity. The "price" of money is its purchasing power in terms of all goods in the economy, and this is determined by its supply, and by every individual's demand for money. Any attempt by government to fix the price will interfere with the satisfaction of people's demands for money. If people find it more convenient to use more than one metal as money, the exchange rate between them on the market will be determined by the relative demands and supplies, and will tend to equal the ratios of their respective purchasing power. Once there is enough supply of a metal to permit the market to choose it as money, no increase in supply can improve its monetary function. An increase in money supply will then merely dilute the effectiveness of each ounce of money without helping the economy. An increased stock of gold or silver, however, fulfills more *non*monetary wants (ornament, industrial purposes, etc.) served by the metal, and is therefore socially useful. Inflation (an increase in money substitutes not covered by an increase in the metal stock) is never socially useful, but merely benefits one set of people at the expense of another. Inflation, being a fraudulent invasion of property, could not take place on the free market.

In sum, freedom can run a monetary system as superbly as it runs the rest of the economy. Contrary to many writers, there is nothing special about money that requires extensive governmental dictation. Here, too, free men will best and most smoothly supply all their economic wants. For money as for all other activities of man, "liberty is the mother, not the daughter, of order."

III.
Government Meddling With Money

1.
The Revenue of Government

Governments, in contrast to all other organizations, do not obtain their revenue as payment for their services. Consequently, governments face an economic problem different from that of everyone else. Private individuals who want to acquire more goods and services from others must produce and sell more of what others want. Governments need only find some method of expropriating more goods without the owner's consent.

In a barter economy, government officials can only expropriate resources in one way: by seizing goods *in kind.* In a monetary economy they will find it easier to seize *monetary* assets, and then use the money to acquire goods and services for government, or else pay the money as subsidies to favored groups. Such seizure is called *taxation*.[1]

Taxation, however, is often unpopular, and, in less temperate days, frequently precipitated revolutions. The emergence of money, while a boon to the human race, also opened a more subtle route for governmental expropriation of resources. On the free market, money can be acquired by producing and selling goods and services that people want, or by mining (a business no more profitable, in the long run, than any other). But if government can find ways to engage in *counterfeiting*—the creation of new money out of thin air—it can quickly produce its own money without taking the trouble to sell services or mine gold. It can then appropriate resources slyly and almost unnoticed, without rousing the hostility touched off by taxation. In fact, counterfeiting can create in its very victims the blissful illusion of unparalleled prosperity.

Counterfeiting is evidently but another name for inflation—both creating new "money" that is not standard gold or silver, and both functioning similarly. And now we see why governments are inherently inflationary: because inflation is a powerful and subtle means for government acquisition of the public's resources, a painless and all the more dangerous form of taxation.

---

[1] Direct seizure of goods is therefore not now as extensive as monetary expropriation. Instances of the former still occurring are "due process" seizure of land under eminent domain, quartering of troops in an occupied country, and especially compulsory confiscation of labor service (e.g., military conscription, compulsory jury duty, and forcing business to keep tax records and collect withholding taxes).

2.
The Economic Effects of Inflation

To gauge the economic effects of inflation, let us see what happens when a group of counterfeiters set about their work. Suppose the economy has a supply of 10,000 gold ounces, and counterfeiters, so cunning that they cannot be detected, pump in 2,000 "ounces" more. What will be the consequences? First, there will be a clear gain to the counterfeiters. They take the newly-created money and use it to buy goods and services. In the words of the famous *New Yorker* cartoon, showing a group of counterfeiters in sober contemplation of their handiwork: "Retail spending is about to get a needed shot in the arm." Precisely. Local spending, indeed, *does* get a shot in the arm. The new money works its way, step by step, throughout the economic system. As the new money spreads, it bids prices up—as we have seen, new money can only dilute the effectiveness of each dollar. But this dilution takes time and is therefore uneven; in the meantime, some people gain and other people lose. In short, the counterfeiters and their local retailers have found their incomes increased before any rise in the prices of the things they buy. But, on the other hand, people in remote areas of the economy, who have not yet received the new money, find their buying prices rising before their incomes. Retailers at the other end of the country, for example, will suffer losses. The first receivers of the new money gain most, and at the expense of the latest receivers.

Inflation, then, confers no general social benefit; instead, it redistributes the wealth in favor of the first-comers and at the expense of the laggards in the race. And inflation is, in effect, a race—to see who can get the new money earliest. The latecomers—the ones stuck with the loss—are often called the "fixed income groups." Ministers, teachers, people on salaries, lag notoriously behind other groups in acquiring the new money. Particular sufferers will be those depending on fixed money contracts—contracts made in the days before the inflationary rise in prices. Life insurance beneficiaries and annuitants, retired persons living off pensions, landlords with long term leases, bondholders and other creditors, those holding cash, all will bear the brunt of the inflation. They will be the ones who are "taxed."[2]

Inflation has other disastrous effects. It distorts that keystone of our economy: business calculation. Since prices do not all change uniformly and at the same speed, it becomes very difficult for business to separate the lasting from the transitional, and gauge truly the demands of consumers or the cost of their operations. For example, accounting practice enters the "cost" of an asset at the amount the business has paid for it. But if inflation intervenes, the cost of replacing the asset

[2] It has become fashionable to scoff at the concern displayed by "conservatives" for the "widows and orphans" hurt by inflation. And yet this is precisely one of the chief problems that must be faced. Is it really "progressive" to rob widows and orphans and to use the proceeds to subsidize farmers and armament workers?

when it wears out will be far greater than that recorded on the books. As a result, business accounting will seriously overstate their profits during inflation—and may even consume capital while presumably increasing their investments.[3] Similarly, stockholders and real estate holders will acquire capital gains during an inflation that are not really "gains" at all. But they may spend part of these gains without realizing that they are thereby consuming their original capital.

By creating illusory profits and distorting economic calculation, inflation will suspend the free market's penalizing of inefficient, and rewarding of efficient, firms. Almost all firms will seemingly prosper. The general atmosphere of a "sellers' market" will lead to a decline in the quality of goods and of service to consumers, since consumers often resist price increases less when they occur in the form of downgrading of quality.[4] The quality of work will decline in an inflation for a more subtle reason: people become enamored of "get-rich-quick" schemes, seemingly within their grasp in an era of ever-rising prices, and often scorn sober effort. Inflation also penalizes thrift and encourages debt, for any sum of money loaned will be repaid in

[3] This error will be greatest in those firms with the oldest equipment, and in the most heavily capitalized industries. An undue number of firms, therefore, will pour into these industries during an inflation. For further discussion of this accounting-cost error, see W.T. Baxter, "The Accountant's Contribution to the Trade Cycle," *Economica* (May 1955): 99–112.

[4] In these days of rapt attention to "cost-of-living indexes" (e.g., escalator-wage contracts) there is strong incentive to increase prices in such a way that the change will not be revealed in the index.

dollars of lower purchasing power than when originally received. The incentive, then, is to borrow and repay later rather than save and lend. Inflation, therefore, lowers the general standard of living in the very course of creating a tinsel atmosphere of "prosperity."

Fortunately, inflation cannot go on forever. For eventually people wake up to this form of taxation; they wake up to the continual shrinkage in the purchasing power of their dollar.

At first, when prices rise, people say: "Well, this is abnormal, the product of some emergency. I will postpone my purchases and wait until prices go back down." This is the common attitude during the first phase of an inflation. This notion moderates the price rise itself, and conceals the inflation further, since the demand for money is thereby increased. But, as inflation proceeds, people begin to realize that prices are going up perpetually as a result of perpetual inflation. Now people will say: "I will buy now, though prices are 'high,' because if I wait, prices will go up still further." As a result, the demand for money now falls and prices go up *more,* proportionately, than the increase in the money supply. At this point, the government is often called upon to "relieve the money shortage" caused by the accelerated price rise, and it inflates even faster. Soon, the country reaches the stage of the "crack-up boom," when people say: "I must buy anything now—anything to get rid of money which depreciates on my hands." The supply of money skyrockets, the demand plummets, and prices rise astronomically. Production falls sharply, as people spend more and more of their time finding ways to get rid of their money. The monetary system has, in effect, broken down completely, and the economy reverts to other moneys, if they are attainable—other metal, foreign currencies if this is a one-country inflation, or even a return to barter conditions. The monetary system has broken down under the impact of inflation.

This condition of *hyper-inflation* is familiar historically in the *assignats* of the French Revolution, the Continentals of the American Revolution, and especially the German crisis of 1923, and the Chinese and other currencies after World War II.[5]

A final indictment of inflation is that whenever the newly issued money is first used as loans to business, inflation causes the dread "business cycle." This silent but deadly process, undetected for generations, works as follows: new money is issued by the banking system, under the aegis of government, and loaned to business. To businessmen, the new funds seem to be genuine investments, but these funds do not, like free-market investments, arise from voluntary savings. The new money is invested by businessmen in various projects, and paid out to workers and other factors as higher wages and prices. As the new money filters down to the whole economy, the people tend to re-establish their old voluntary consumption/saving proportions.

---

[5] On the German example, see Costantino Bresciani-Turroni, *The Economics of Inflation* (London: George Allen and Unwin, 1937).

In short, if people wish to save and invest about 20 percent of their incomes and consume the rest, new bank money loaned to business at first makes the saving proportion look higher. When the new money seeps down to the public, it re-establishes its old 20–80 proportion, and many investments are now revealed to be wasteful. Liquidation of the wasteful investments of the inflationary boom constitutes the *depression* phase of the business cycle.[6]

3. Compulsory Monopoly of the Mint

For government to use counterfeiting to add to its revenue, many lengthy steps must be travelled down the road away from the free market. Government could not simply invade a functioning free market and print its own paper tickets. Done so abruptly, few people would accept the government's money. Even in modern times, many people in "backward countries" have simply refused to accept paper money, and insist on trading only in gold. Governmental incursion, therefore, must be far more subtle and gradual.

Until a few centuries ago, there were no banks, and therefore the government could not use the banking engine for massive inflation as it can today. What could it do when only gold and silver circulated?

---

[6] For a further discussion, see Murray N. Rothbard, *America's Great Depression* (Princeton, N.J.: D. Van Nostrand, 1963), Part I.

The first step, taken firmly by every sizeable government, was to seize an absolute monopoly of the *minting* business. That was the indispensable means of getting control of the coinage supply. The king's or the lord's picture was stamped upon coins, and the myth was propagated that coinage is an essential prerogative of royal or baronial "sovereignty." The mintage monopoly allowed government to supply whatever denominations of coin it, and not the public, wanted. As a result, the variety of coins on the market was forcibly reduced. Furthermore, the mint could now charge a high price, greater than costs ("seigniorage"), a price just covering costs ("brassage"), or supply coins free of charge. Seigniorage was a monopoly price, and it imposed a special burden on the conversion of bullion to coin; gratuitous coinage, on the other hand, overstimulated the manufacture of coins from bullion, and forced the general taxpayer to pay for minting services utilized by others.

Having acquired the mintage monopoly, governments fostered the use of the *name* of the monetary unit, doing their best to separate the name from its true base in the underlying weight of the coin. This, too, was a highly important step, for it liberated each government from the necessity of abiding by the common money of the world market. Instead of using grains or grams of gold or silver, each State fostered its own national name in the supposed interests of monetary patriotism: dollars, marks, francs, and the like. The shift made possible the preeminent means of governmental counterfeiting of coin: debasement.

4.
Debasement

Debasement was the State's method of counterfeiting the very coins it had banned private firms from making in the name of vigorous protection of the monetary standard. Sometimes, the government committed simple fraud, secretly diluting gold with a base alloy, making shortweight coins. More characteristically, the mint melted and recoined all the coins of the realm, giving the subjects back the same number of "pounds" or "marks," but of a lighter weight. The leftover ounces of gold or silver were pocketed by the King and used to pay his expenses. In that way, government continually juggled and redefined the very standard it was pledged to protect. The profits of debasement were haughtily claimed as "seigniorage" by the rulers.

Rapid and severe debasement was a hallmark of the Middle Ages, in almost every country in Europe. Thus, in 1200 A.D., the French *livre tournois* was defined at ninety-eight grams of fine silver; by 1600 A.D. it signified only eleven grams. A striking case is the *dinar,* a coin of the Saracens in Spain. The *dinar* originally consisted of sixty-five gold grains, when first coined at the end of the seventh century. The Saracens were notably sound in monetary matters, and by the middle of the twelfth century, the *dinar* was still sixty grains. At that point, the Christian kings conquered Spain, and by the early thirteenth century, the *dinar* (now called *maravedi*) was reduced to fourteen grains. Soon the gold coin was too light to circulate, and it was converted into a *silver* coin weighing twenty-six grains of silver. This, too, was debased, and by the mid-fifteenth century, the *maravedi* was only 1.5 silver grains, and again too small to circulate.[7]

5. Gresham's Law and Coinage

A. Bimetallism

Government imposes price controls largely in order to divert public attention from governmental inflation to the alleged evils of the free market. As we have seen, "Gresham's Law"—that an artificially overvalued money tends to drive an artificially undervalued money out of circulation—is an example of the general consequences of price control. Government places, in effect, a maximum price on one type of money in terms of the other. Maximum price causes a shortage—disappearance into hoards or exports—of the currency suffering the maximum price (artificially undervalued), and leads it to be replaced in circulation by the overpriced money.

We have seen how this works in the case of new versus worn coins, one of the earliest examples of Gresham's Law. Changing the meaning of money from weight to mere tale, and standardizing denominations

---

[7] On debasement, see Elgin Groseclose, *Money and Man* (New York: Frederick Ungar, 1961), pp. 57–76.

for their own rather than for the public's convenience, the governments called new and worn coins by the same name, even though they were of different weight. As a result, people hoarded or exported the full weight new coins, and passed the worn coins in circulation, with governments hurling maledictions at "speculators," foreigners, or the free market in general, for a condition brought about by the government itself.

A particularly important case of Gresham's Law was the perennial problem of the "standard." We saw that the free market established "parallel standards" of gold and silver, each freely fluctuating in relation to the other in accordance with market supplies and demands. But governments decided they would help out the market by stepping in to "simplify" matters. How much clearer things would be, they felt, if gold and silver were fixed at a definite ratio, say, twenty ounces of silver to one ounce of gold! Then, both moneys could always circulate at a fixed ratio—and, far more importantly, the government could finally rid itself of the burden of treating money by weight instead of by tale. Let us imagine a unit, the "rur," defined by Ruritanians as 1/20 of an ounce of gold. We have seen how vital it is for the government to induce the public to regard the "rur" as an abstract unit of its own right, only loosely connected to gold. What better way of doing this than to fix the gold/silver ratio? Then, "rur" becomes not only 1/20 ounce of gold, *but also* one ounce of silver. The precise meaning of the word "rur"—a name for gold weight—is now lost, and people begin to think of the "rur" as something tangible in its own right, somehow set by the government, for good and efficient purposes, as equal to certain weights of both gold and silver.

Now we see the importance of abstaining from patriotic or national names for gold ounces or grains. Once such a label replaces the recognized world units of weight, it becomes much easier for governments to manipulate the money unit and give it an apparent life of its own. The fixed gold-silver ration, known as *bimetallism,* accomplished this task very neatly. It did *not,* however, fulfill its other job of simplifying the nation's currency. For, once again, Gresham's Law came into prominence. The government usually set the bimetallic ration originally (say, 20/1) at the going rate on the free market. But the market ratio, like all market prices, inevitably changes over time, as supply and demand conditions change. As changes occur, the fixed bimetallic ratio inevitably becomes obsolete. Change makes either gold or silver overvalued. Gold then disappears into cash balance, black market, or exports, when silver flows in from abroad and comes out of cash balances to become the only circulating currency in Ruritania. For centuries, all countries struggled with calamitous effects of suddenly alternating metallic currencies. First silver would flow in and gold disappear; then, as the relative market ratios changed, gold would pour in and silver disappear.[8]

[8] Many debasements, in fact, occurred covertly, with governments claiming that they were merely bringing the official gold-silver ratio into closer alignment with the market.

Finally, after weary centuries of bimetallic disruption, governments picked one metal as the standard, generally gold. Silver was relegated to "token coin" status, for small denominations, but not at full weight. (The minting of token coins was also monopolized by government, and, since not backed 100 percent by gold, was a means of expanding the money supply.) The eradication of silver as money certainly injured many people who preferred to use silver for various transactions. There was truth in the warcry of the bimetallists that a "crime against silver" had been committed; but the crime was really the original imposition of bimetallism in lieu of parallel standards. Bimetallism created an impossibly difficult situation, which the government could either meet by going back to full monetary freedom (parallel standards) or by picking one of the two metals as money (gold or silver standard). Full monetary freedom, after all this time, was considered absurd and quixotic; and so the gold standard was generally adopted.

B. Legal Tender

How was the government able to enforce its price controls on monetary exchange rates? By a device known as *legal tender laws*. Money is used for payment of past debts, as well as for present "cash" transactions. With the name of the country's currency now prominent in accounting instead its actual weight, contracts began to pledge payment in certain amounts of "money." *Legal tender laws* dictated what that "money" could be. When only the original gold or silver was designated "legal tender," people considered it harmless, but they should have realized that a dangerous precedent had been set for government control of money. If the government sticks to the original money, its legal tender law is superfluous and unnecessary.[9] On the other hand, the government may declare as legal tender a lower-quality currency side-by-side with the original. Thus, the government may decree worn coins as good as new ones in paying off debt, or silver and gold equivalent to each other in the fixed ratio. The legal tender laws then bring Gresham's Law into being.

When legal tender laws enshrine an overvalued money, they have another effect; they favor debtors at the expense of creditors. For then debtors are permitted to pay back their debts in a much poorer money than they had borrowed, and creditors are swindled out of the money rightfully theirs. This confiscation of creditors property, however, only benefits outstanding debtors; *future* debtors will be burdened by the scarcity

---

[9] Lord Farrer, *Studies in Currency 1898* (London: Macmillan, 1898), p. 43.

> The ordinary law of contract does all that is necessary without any law giving special functions to particular forms of currency. We have adopted a gold sovereign as our unit. . . . If I promise to pay 100 sovereigns, it needs no special currency law of legal tender to say that I am bound to pay 100 sovereigns, and that, if required to pay the 100 sovereigns, I cannot discharge my obligation by paying anything else.

On the legal tender laws, see also Ludwig von Mises, *Human Action* (New Haven, Conn.: Yale University Press, 1949), pp. 432n. and 444.

of credit generated by the memory of government spoliation of creditors.

6. Summary: Government and Coinage

The compulsory minting monopoly and legal tender legislation were the capstones in governments' drive to gain control of their nations' money. Bolstering these measures, each government moved to abolish the circulation of all coins minted by rival governments.[10] Within each country, only the coin of its own sovereign could now be used; between countries, unstamped gold and silver bullion was used in exchange. This further severed the ties between the various parts of the world market, further sundering one country from another, and disrupting the international division of labor. Yet, purely hard money did not leave too much scope for governmental inflation. There were limits to the debasing that governments could engineer, and the fact that all countries used gold and silver placed definite checks on the control of each government over its own territory. The rulers were still held in check by the discipline of an international metallic money.

Governmental control of money could only become absolute, and its counterfeiting unchallenged, as

[10] The use of foreign coins was prevalent in the Middle Ages and in the United States down to the middle of the nineteenth century.

money-substitutes came into prominence in recent centuries. The advent of paper money and bank deposits, an economic boon when backed fully by gold or silver, provided the open sesame for government's road to power over money, and thereby over the entire economic system.

7.
Permitting Banks to Refuse Payment

The modern economy, with its widespread use of banks and money-substitutes, provides the golden opportunity for government to fasten its control over the money supply and permit inflation at its discretion. We have seen in section 12, page 38, that there are three great checks on the power of any bank to inflate under a "free-banking" system: (1) the extent of the clientele of each bank; (2) the extent of the clientele of the whole banking system, i.e., the extent to which people use money-substitutes; and (3) the confidence of the clients in their banks. The narrower the clientele of each bank, of the banking system as a whole, or the shakier the state of confidence, the stricter will be the limits on inflation in the economy. Government's privileging and controlling of the banking system has operated to suspend these limits.

All these limits, of course, rest on one fundamental obligation: the duty of the banks to redeem their sworn liabilities on demand. We have seen that no fractional-reserve bank can redeem all of its liabilities; and we have also seen that this is the gamble that every bank takes. But it is, of course, essential to any system of private property that contract obligations be fulfilled. The bluntest way for government to foster inflation, then, is to grant the banks the special privilege of refusing to pay their obligations, while yet continuing in their operation. While everyone else must pay their debts or go bankrupt, the banks are permitted to refuse redemption of their receipts, at the same time forcing their own debtors to pay when their loans fall due. The usual name for this is a "suspension of specie payments." A more accurate name would be "license for theft;" for what else can we call a governmental permission to continue in business without fulfilling one's contract?

In the United States, mass suspension of specie payment in times of bank troubles became almost a tradition. It started in the War of 1812. Most of the country's banks were located in New England, a section unsympathetic to America's entry into the war. These banks refused to lend for war purposes, and so the government borrowed from new banks in the other states. These banks issued new paper money to make the loans. The inflation was so great that calls for redemption flooded into the new banks, especially from the conservative nonexpanding banks of New England, where the government spent most of its money on war goods. As a result, there was a mass "suspension" in 1814, lasting for over two years (well beyond the end of the war); during that time, banks sprouted up, issuing notes with no need to redeem in gold or silver.

This suspension set a precedent for succeeding economic crises; 1819, 1837, 1857, and so forth. As a result of this tradition, the banks realized that they need have no fear of bankruptcy after an inflation, and this, of course, stimulated inflation and "wildcat banking." Those writers who point to nineteenth century America as a horrid example of "free banking," fail to realize the importance of this clear dereliction of duty by the states in every financial crisis.

The governments and the banks, persuaded the public of the justice of their acts. In fact, anyone trying to get his money back during a crisis was considered "unpatriotic" and a despoiler of his fellowmen, while banks were often commended for patriotically bailing out the community in a time of trouble. Many people, however, were bitter at the entire proceeding and from this sentiment grew the famous "hard money" Jacksonian movement that flourished before the Civil War.[11]

Despite its use in the United States, such periodic privilege to banks did not catch hold as a general policy in the modern world. It was a crude instrument, too sporadic (it could not be permanent since few people would patronize banks that never paid their obligations)—and, what's more, it provided no means of

[11] See Horace White, *Money and Banking,* 4th ed. (Boston: Ginn, 1911), pp. 322–27.

government control over the banking system. What governments want, after all, is not simply inflation, but inflation completely controlled and directed by themselves. There must be no danger of the banks running the show. And so, a far subtler, smoother, more permanent method was devised, and sold to the public as a hallmark of civilization itself—Central Banking.

8. Central Banking: Removing the Checks on Inflation

Central Banking is now put in the same class with modern plumbing and good roads: any economy that doesn't have it is called "backward," "primitive," hopelessly out of the swim. America's adoption of the Federal Reserve System—our Central Bank—in 1913 was greeted as finally putting us in the ranks of the "advanced" nations.

Central Banks are often nominally owned by private individuals or, as in the United States, jointly by private banks; but they are always directed by government-appointed officials, and serve as arms of the government. Where they are privately owned, as in the original Bank of England or the Second Bank of the United States, their prospective profits add to the usual governmental desire for inflation.

A Central Bank attains its commanding position from its governmentally granted *monopoly of the note issue.* This is often the unsung key to its power.

Invariably, private banks are prohibited from issuing notes, and the privilege is reserved to the Central Bank. The private banks can only grant deposits. If their customers ever wish to shift from deposits to notes, therefore, the banks must go to the Central Bank to get them. Hence the Central Bank's lofty perch as a "bankers' bank." It is a bankers' bank because the bankers are forced to do business with it. As a result, bank deposits became redeemable not only in gold, but also in Central Bank notes. And these new notes were not just plain bank notes. They were liabilities of the Central Bank, an institution invested with all the majestic aura of the government itself. Government, after all, appoints the Bank officials and coordinates its policy with other state policy. It receives the notes in taxes, and declares them to be legal tender.

As a result of these measures, all the banks in the country became clients of the Central Bank.[12] Gold poured into the Central Bank from the private banks, and, in exchange, the public got Central Bank notes and the disuse of gold coins. Gold coins were scoffed at by "official" opinion as cumbersome, old-fashioned, inefficient—an ancient "fetish," perhaps useful in children's socks at Christmas, but that's about all. How much safer, more convenient, more efficient is the gold when resting as bullion in the mighty vaults of the Central

[12] In the United States, the banks were forced by law to join the Federal Reserve System, and to keep their accounts with the Federal Reserve Banks. (Those "state banks" that are not members of the Federal Reserve System keep their reserves with member banks.)

Bank! Bathed by this propaganda, and influenced by the convenience and governmental backing of the notes, the public more and more stopped using gold coins in its daily life. Inexorably, the gold flowed into the Central Bank where, more "centralized," it permitted a far greater degree of inflation of money-substitutes.

In the United States, the Federal Reserve Act compels the banks to keep the minimum ratio of reserves to deposits and, since 1917, these reserves could only consist of deposits at the Federal Reserve Bank. Gold could no longer be part of a bank's legal reserves; it had to be deposited in the Federal Reserve Bank.

The entire process took the public off the gold habit and placed the people's gold in the none-too-tender care of the State—where it could be confiscated almost painlessly. International traders still used gold bullion in their large-scale transactions, but they were an insignificant proportion of the voting population.

One of the reasons the public could be lured from gold to bank notes was the great *confidence* everyone had in the Central Bank. Surely, the Central Bank, possessed of almost all the gold in the realm, backed by the might and prestige of government, could not fail and go bankrupt! And it is certainly true that no Central Bank in recorded history has ever failed. But why not? Because of the sometimes unwritten but very clear rule that it *could not* be permitted to fail! If governments sometimes allowed private banks to suspend payment, how much more readily would it permit the Central Bank—its own organ—to suspend when in trouble! The precedent was set in Central Banking history when England permitted the Bank of England to suspend in the late eighteenth century, and allowed this suspension for over twenty years.

The Central Bank thus became armed with the almost unlimited confidence of the public. By this time, the public could not see that the Central Bank was being allowed to counterfeit at will, and yet remain immune from any liability if its bona fides should be questioned. It came to see the Central Bank as simply a great national bank, performing a public service, and protected from failure by being a virtual arm of the government.

The Central Bank proceeded to invest the private banks with the public's confidence. This was a more difficult task. The Central Bank let it be known that it would always act as a "lender of last resort" to the banks—i.e., that the Bank would stand ready to lend money to any bank in trouble, especially when many banks are called upon to pay their obligations.

Governments also continued to prop up banks by discouraging bank "runs" (i.e., cases where many clients suspect chicanery and ask to get back their property). Sometimes, they will permitted banks to suspend payment, as in the compulsory bank "holidays" of 1933. Laws were passed prohibiting public encouragement of bank runs, and, as in the 1929 depression in America, government campaigned against "selfish" and "unpatriotic" gold "hoarders." America finally "solved" its pesky problem of bank failures when it adopted Federal Deposit Insurance in 1933. The Federal Deposit Insurance Corporation has only a negligible proportion of "backing" for the bank deposits it "insures." But the public has been given the impression (and one that may well be accurate) that the federal government would stand ready to print enough new money to redeem all of the insured deposits. As a result, the government has managed to transfer its own command of vast public confidence to the entire banking system, as well as to the Central Bank.

We have seen that, by setting up a Central Bank, governments have greatly widened, if not removed, two of the three main checks on bank credit inflation. What of the third check—the problem of the narrowness of each bank's clientele? Removal of this check is one of the main reasons for the Central Bank's existence. In a free-banking system, inflation by any one bank would soon lead to demands for redemption by the other banks, since the clientele of any one bank is severely limited. But the Central Bank, by pumping reserves into all the banks, can make sure that they can all expand together, and at a uniform rate. If all banks are expanding, then there is no redemption problem of one bank upon another, and each bank finds that its clientele is really the whole country. In short, the limits on bank expansion are immeasurably widened, from the clientele of each bank to that of the whole banking system. Of course, this means that no bank can expand further than the Central Bank desires. Thus, the government has finally achieved the power to control and direct the inflation of the banking system.

In addition to removing the checks on inflation, the act of establishing a Central Bank has a direct inflationary impact. Before the Central Bank began, banks kept their reserves in gold; now gold flows into the Central Bank in exchange for deposits with the Bank, which are now reserves for the commercial banks. But the Bank itself keeps only a fractional reserve of gold to its own liabilities! Therefore, the act of establishing a Central Bank greatly multiplies the inflationary potential of the country.[13]

9.
Central Banking: Directing the Inflation

Precisely how does the Central Bank go about its task of regulating the private banks? By controlling the banks' "reserves"—their deposit accounts at the Central Bank. Banks tend to keep a certain ratio of reserves to their total deposit liabilities, and in the United States government control is made easier by imposing a legal minimum ratio on the bank. The Central Bank can stimulate inflation, then, by pouring reserves into the

---

[13] The establishment of the Federal Reserve in this way increased threefold the expansive power of the banking system of the United States. The Federal Reserve System also reduced the average legal reserve requirements of all banks from approximately 21 percent in 1913 to 10 percent by 1917, thus further doubling the inflationary potential—a combined potential inflation of six-fold. See Chester A. Phillips, T.F. McManus, and R.W. Nelson, *Banking and the Business Cycle* (New York: Macmillan, 1937), pp. 23ff.

banking system, and also by lowering the reserve ratio, thus permitting a nationwide bank credit-expansion. If the banks keep a reserve/deposit ratio of 1:10, then "excess reserves" (above the required ratio) of ten million dollars will permit and encourage a nationwide bank inflation of 100 million. Since banks profit by credit expansion, and since government has made it almost impossible for them to fail, they will usually try to keep "loaned up" to their allowable maximum.

The Central Bank adds to the quantity of bank reserves by buying assets on the market. What happens, for example, if the Bank buys an asset (any asset) from Mr. Jones, valued at $1,000? The Central Bank writes out a check to Mr. Jones for $1,000 to pay for the asset. The Central Bank does not keep individual accounts, so Mr. Jones takes the check and deposits it in his bank. Jones' bank credits him with a $1,000 deposit, and presents the check to the Central Bank, which has to credit the bank with an added $1,000 in reserves. This $1,000 in reserves permits a multiple bank credit expansion, particularly if added reserves are in this way poured into many banks across the country.

If the Central Bank buys an asset from a bank directly, then the result is even clearer; the bank adds to its reserves, and a base for multiple credit expansion is established.

Undoubtedly, the favorite asset for Central Bank purchase has been government securities. In that way, the government assures a market for its own securities. Government can easily inflate the money supply by issuing new bonds, and then order its Central Bank to purchase them. Often the Central Bank undertakes to support the market price of government securities at a certain level, thereby causing a flow of securities into the Bank, and a consequent perpetual inflation.

Besides buying assets, the Central Bank can create new bank reserves in another way: by lending them. The rate which the Central Bank charges the banks for this service is the "rediscount rate." Clearly, borrowed reserves are not as satisfactory to the banks as reserves that are wholly theirs, since there is now pressure for repayment. Changes in the rediscount rate receive a great deal of publicity, but they are clearly of minor importance compared to the movements in the quantity of bank reserves and the reserve ratio.

When the Central Bank sells assets to the banks or the public, it lowers bank reserves, and causes pressure for credit contraction and deflation—lowering—of the money supply. We have seen, however, that governments are inherently inflationary; historically, deflationary action by the government has been negligible and fleeting. One thing is often forgotten: deflation can only take place after a previous inflation; only pseudo-receipts, not gold coins, can be retired and liquidated.

10. Going Off the Gold Standard

The establishment of Central Banking removes the checks of bank credit expansion, and puts the inflationary engine into operation. It does not remove all restraints, however. There is still the problem of the Central Bank itself. The citizens can conceivably make a run on the Central Bank, but this is most improbable. A more formidable threat is the loss of gold to foreign nations. For just as the expansion of one bank loses gold to the clients of other, nonexpanding banks, so does monetary expansion in one country cause a loss of gold to the citizens of other countries. Countries that expand faster are in danger of gold losses and calls upon their banking system for gold redemption. This was the classic cyclical pattern of the nineteenth century; a country's Central Bank would generate bank credit expansion; prices would rise; and as the new money spread from domestic to foreign clientele, foreigners would more and more try to redeem the currency in gold. Finally, the Central Bank would have to call a halt and enforce a credit contraction in order to save the monetary standard.

There is one way that foreign redemption can be avoided: inter-Central Bank cooperation. If all Central Banks agree to inflate at about the same rate, then no country would lose gold to any other, and all the world together could inflate almost without limit. With every government jealous of its own power and responsive to different pressures, however, such goose-step cooperation has so far proved almost impossible. One of the closest approaches was the American Federal Reserve agreement to promote domestic inflation in the 1920s in order to help Great Britain and prevent it from losing gold to the United States.

In the twentieth century, governments, rather than deflate or limit their own inflation, have simply "gone off the gold standard" when confronted with heavy demands for gold. This, of course, insures that the Central Bank cannot fail, since its notes now become the standard money. In short, government has finally refused to pay its debts, and has virtually absolved the banking system from that onerous duty. Pseudo-receipts to gold were first issued without backing and then, when the day of reckoning drew near, the bankruptcy was shamelessly completed by simply eliminating gold redemption. The severance of the various national currency names (dollar, pound, mark) from gold and silver is now complete.

At first, governments refused to admit that this was a permanent measure. They referred to the "suspension of specie payments," and it was always understood that eventually, after the war or other "emergency" had ended, the government would again redeem its obligations. When the Bank of England went off gold at the end of the eighteenth century, it continued in this state for twenty years, but always with the understanding that gold payment would be resumed after the French wars were ended.

Temporary "suspensions," however, are primrose paths to outright repudiation. The gold standard, after all, is no spigot that can be turned on or off as government whim decrees. Either a gold-receipt is redeemable or it is not; once redemption is suspended the gold standard is itself a mockery.

Another step in the slow extinction of gold money was the establishment of the "gold bullion standard." Under this system, the currency is no longer redeemable in coins; it can only be redeemed in large, highly valuable, gold bars. This, in effect, limits gold redemption to a handful of specialists in foreign trade. There is no longer a true gold standard, but governments can still proclaim their adherence to gold. The European "gold standards" of the 1920s were pseudo-standards of this type.[14]

Finally, governments went "off gold" officially and completely, in a thunder of abuse against foreigners and "unpatriotic gold hoarders." Government paper now becomes the *fiat* standard money. Sometimes, Treasury rather than Central Bank paper has been the fiat money, especially before the development of a Central Banking system. The American Continentals, the Greenbacks, and Confederate notes of the Civil War period, the French *assignats,* were all fiat currencies issued by the Treasuries. But whether Treasury or Central Bank, the effect of fiat issue is the same: the monetary standard is now at the mercy of the government, and bank deposits are redeemable simply in government paper.

11. Fiat Money and the Gold Problem

When a country goes off the gold standard and onto the fiat standard, it adds to the number of

[14] See Melchior Palyi, "The Meaning of the Gold Standard," *Journal of Business* (July 1941): 299–304.

"moneys" in existence. In addition to the commodity moneys, gold and silver, there now flourish independent moneys directed by each government imposing its fiat rule. And just as gold and silver will have an exchange rate on the free market, so the market will establish exchange rates for all the various moneys. In a world of fiat moneys, each currency, if permitted, will fluctuate freely in relation to all the others. We have seen that for any two moneys, the exchange rate is set in accordance with the proportionate purchasing-power parities, and that these in turn are determined by the respective supplies and demands for the various currencies. When a currency changes its character from gold-receipt to fiat paper, confidence in its stability and quality is shaken, and demand for it declines. Furthermore, now that it is cut off from gold, its far greater quantity relative to its former gold backing now becomes evident. With a supply greater than gold and a lower demand, its purchasing-power, and hence its exchange rate, quickly depreciate in relation to gold. And since government is inherently inflationary, it will keep depreciating as time goes on.

Such depreciation is highly embarrassing to the government—and hurts citizens who try to import goods. The existence of gold in the economy is a constant reminder of the poor quality of the government paper, and it always poses a threat to replace the paper as the country's money. Even with the government giving all the backing of its prestige and its legal tender laws to its fiat paper, gold coins in the hands of the public will always be a permanent reproach and menace to the government's power over the country's money.

In America's first depression, 1819–1821, four Western states (Tennessee, Kentucky, Illinois, and Missouri) established state-owned banks, issuing fiat paper. They were backed by legal tender provisions in the states, and sometimes by legal prohibition against depreciating the notes. And yet, all these experiments, born in high hopes, came quickly to grief as the new paper depreciated rapidly to negligible value. The projects had to be swiftly abandoned. Later, the greenbacks circulated as fiat paper in the North during and after the Civil War. Yet, in California, the people refused to accept the greenbacks and continued to use gold as their money. As a prominent economist pointed out:

> In California, as in other states, the paper was legal tender and was receivable for public dues; nor was there any distrust or hostility toward the federal government. But there was a strong feeling . . . in favor of gold and against paper. . . . Every debtor had the legal right to pay off his debts in depreciated paper. But if he did so, he was a marked man (the creditor was likely to post him publicly in the newspapers) and he was virtually boycotted. Throughout this period paper was not used in California. The people of the state

> conducted their transactions in gold, while all the rest of the United States used convertible paper.[15]

It became clear to governments that they could not afford to allow people to own and keep their gold. Government could never cement its power over a nation's currency, if the people, when in need, could repudiate the fiat paper and turn to gold for their money. Accordingly, governments have outlawed gold holding by their citizens. Gold, except for a negligible amount permitted for industrial and ornamental purposes, has generally been nationalized. To ask for return of the public's confiscated property is now considered hopelessly backward and old-fashioned.[16]

12.
Fiat Money and Gresham's Law

With fiat money established and gold outlawed, the way is clear for full-scale, government-run inflation. Only one very broad check remains: the ultimate threat of hyper-inflation, the crack-up of the currency. Hyper-inflation occurs when the public realizes that the government is bent on inflation, and decides to evade

---

[15] Frank W. Taussig, *Principles of Economics,* 2nd ed. (New York: Macmillan, 1916), vol. I, p. 312. Also see J.K. Upton, *Money in Politics,* 2nd ed. (Boston: Lothrop Publishing, 1895), pp. 69 ff.

[16] For an incisive analysis of the steps by which the American government confiscated the people's gold and went off the gold standard in 1933, see Garet Garrett, *The People's Pottage* (Caldwell, Idaho: Caxton Printers, 1953), pp. 15–41.

the inflationary tax on its resources by spending money as fast as possible while it still retains some value. Until hyper-inflation sets in, however, government can now manage the currency and the inflation undisturbed. New difficulties arise, however. As always, government intervention to cure one problem raises a host of new, unexpected problems. In a world of fiat moneys, each country has its own money. The international division of labor, based on an international currency, has been broken, and countries tend to divide into their own autarchic units. Lack of monetary certainty disrupts trade further. The standard of living in each country thereby declines. Each country has freely-fluctuating exchange rates with all other currencies. A country inflating beyond the others no longer fears a loss of gold; but it faces other unpleasant consequences. The exchange rate of its currency falls in relation to foreign currencies. This is not only embarrassing but even disturbing to citizens who fear further depreciation. It also greatly raises the costs of imported goods, and this means a great deal to those countries with a high proportion of international trade.

In recent years, therefore, governments have moved to abolish freely-fluctuating exchange rates. Instead, they fixed arbitrary exchange rates with other currencies. Gresham's Law tells us precisely the result of any such arbitrary price control. Whatever rate is set will not be the free-market one, since that can be only be determined from day-to-day on the market. Therefore, one currency will always be artificially overvalued and the other, undervalued. Generally, governments have deliberately overvalued their currencies—for prestige reasons, and also because of the consequences that follow. When a currency is overvalued by decree, people rush to exchange it for the undervalued currency at the bargain rates; this causes a surplus of overvalued, and a shortage of the undervalued, currency. The rate, in short, is prevented from moving to clear the exchange market. In the present world, foreign currencies have generally been overvalued relative to the dollar. The result has been the famous phenomenon of the "dollar shortage"—another testimony to the operation of Gresham's Law.

Foreign countries, clamoring about a "dollar shortage," thus brought it about by their own policies. It is possible that these governments actually welcomed this state of affairs, for (a) it gave them an excuse to clamor for American dollar aid to "relieve the dollar shortage in the free world," and (b) it gave them an excuse to ration imports from America. Undervaluing dollars causes imports from America to be artificially cheap and exports to America artificially expensive. The result: a trade deficit and worry over the dollar drain.[17] The foreign government then stepped in to tell its people sadly that it is unfortunately necessary for it to ration imports: to issue licenses to importers, and determine what is imported "according to need."

[17] In the last few years, the dollar has been overvalued in relation to other currencies, and hence the dollar drains *from* the U.S.

To ration imports, many governments confiscate the foreign exchange holdings of their citizens, backing up an artificially high valuation on domestic currency by forcing these citizens to accept far less domestic money than they could have acquired on the free market. Thus, foreign exchange, as well as gold, has been nationalized, and exporters penalized. In countries where foreign trade is vitally important, this government "exchange control" imposes virtual socialization on the economy. An artificial exchange rate thus gives countries an excuse for demanding foreign aid and for imposing socialist controls over trade.[18]

At present, the world is enmeshed in a chaotic welter of exchange controls, currency blocs, restrictions on convertibility, and multiple systems of rates. In some countries a "black market" in foreign exchange is legally encouraged to find out the true rate, and multiple discriminatory rates are fixed for different types of transactions. Almost all nations are on a fiat standard, but they have not had the courage to admit this outright, and so they proclaim some such fiction as "restricted gold bullion standard." Actually, gold is used not as a true definition for currencies, but as a convenience by governments: for (a) fixing a currency's rate with respect to gold makes it easy to reckon any exchange in terms of any other currency; and (b) gold is still used by the different governments. Since exchange

---

[18] For an excellent discussion of foreign exchange and exchange controls, see George Winder, *The Free Convertibility of Sterling* (London: Batchworth Press, 1955).

rates are fixed, *some* item must move to balance every country's payments, and gold is the ideal candidate. In short gold is no longer the world's money; it is now the *governments'* money, used in payments to one another.

Clearly, the inflationists' dream is some sort of world paper money, manipulated by a world government and Central Bank, inflating everywhere at a common rate. This dream still lies in the dim future, however; we are still far from world government, and national currency problems have so far been too diverse and conflicting to permit meshing into a single unit. Yet, the world has moved steadily in this direction. The International Monetary Fund, for example, is basically an institution designed to bolster national exchange control in general, and foreign undervaluation of the dollar in particular. The Fund requires each member country to fix its exchange rate, and then to pool gold and dollars to lend to governments that find themselves short of hard currency.

13. Government and Money

Many people believe that the free market, despite some admitted advantages, is a picture of disorder and chaos. Nothing is "planned," everything is haphazard. Government dictation, on the other hand, seems simple and orderly; decrees are handed down and they are obeyed. In no area of the economy is this myth more prevalent than in the field of money. Seemingly, money, at least, must come under stringent government control. But money is the lifeblood of the economy; it is the medium for all transactions. If government dictates over money, it has already captured a vital command post for control over the economy, and has secured a stepping-stone for full socialism. We have seen that a free market in money, contrary to common assumption, would not be chaotic; that, in fact, it would be a model of order and efficiency.

What, then, have we learned about government and money? We have seen that, over the centuries, government has, step by step, invaded the free market and seized complete control over the monetary system. We have seen that each new control, sometimes seemingly innocuous, has begotten new and further controls. We have seen that governments are inherently inflationary, since inflation is a tempting means of acquiring revenue for the State and its favored groups. The slow but certain seizure of the monetary reins has thus been used to (a) inflate the economy at a pace decided by government; and (b) bring about socialistic direction of the entire economy.

Furthermore, government meddling with money has not only brought untold tyranny into the world; it has also brought chaos and not order. It has fragmented the peaceful, productive world market and shattered it into a thousand pieces, with trade and investment hobbled and hampered by myriad restrictions, controls, artificial rates, currency breakdowns, etc. It has helped bring about wars by transforming a world of peaceful intercourse into a jungle of warring currency blocs. In short, we find that coercion, in money as in other matters, brings, not order, but conflict and chaos.

IV.
The Monetary Breakdown of the West

Since the first edition of this book was written, the chickens of the monetary interventionists have come home to roost. The world monetary crisis of February–March, 1973, followed by the dollar plunge of July, was only the latest of an accelerating series of crises which provide a virtual textbook illustration of our analysis of the inevitable consequences of government intervention in the monetary system. After each crisis is temporarily allayed by a "Band-Aid" solution, the governments of the West loudly announce that the world monetary system has now been placed on sure footing, and that all the monetary crises have been solved. President Nixon went so far as to call the Smithsonian Agreement of December 18, 1971, the "greatest monetary agreement in the history of the world," only to see this greatest agreement collapse in a little over a year. Each "solution" has crumbled more rapidly than its predecessor. To understand the current monetary chaos, it is necessary to trace briefly the international monetary developments of the twentieth century, and to see how each set of unsound inflationist interventions has collapsed of its own inherent problems, only to set the stage for another round of interventions. The twentieth century history of the world monetary order can be divided into nine phases. Let us examine each in turn.

1.
Phase I:
The Classical Gold Standard, 1815–1914

We can look back upon the "classical" gold standard, the Western world of the nineteenth and early twentieth centuries, as the literal and metaphorical Golden Age. With the exception of the troublesome problem of silver, the world was on a gold standard, which meant that each national currency (the dollar, pound, franc, etc.) was merely a *name* for a certain definite *weight* of gold. The "dollar," for example, was defined as 1/20 of a gold ounce, the pound sterling as slightly less than ¼ of a gold ounce, and so on. This meant that the "exchange rates" between the various national currencies were fixed, not because they were arbitrarily controlled by government, but in the same way that one pound of weight is defined as being equal to sixteen ounces.

The international gold standard meant that the benefits of having one money medium were extended throughout the world. One of the reasons for the growth and prosperity of the United States has been the fact that we have enjoyed one money throughout the large area of the country. We have had a gold or at least a single dollar standard within the entire country, and did not have to suffer the chaos of each city and county issuing its own money which would then fluctuate with respect to the moneys of all the other cities and counties. The nineteenth century saw the benefits of one money throughout the civilized world. One money facilitated freedom of trade, investment, and travel throughout that trading and monetary area, with the consequent growth of specialization and the international division of labor.

It must be emphasized that gold was not selected arbitrarily by governments to be the monetary standard. Gold had developed for many centuries on the free market as the best money; as the commodity providing the most stable and desirable monetary medium. Above all, the supply and provision of gold was subject only to market forces, and not to the arbitrary printing press of the government.

The international gold standard provided an automatic market mechanism for checking the inflationary potential of government. It also provided an automatic mechanism for keeping the balance of payments of each country in equilibrium. As the philosopher and economist David Hume pointed out in the mid-eighteenth century, if one nation, say France, inflates its supply of paper francs, its prices rise; the increasing incomes in paper francs stimulate imports from abroad, which are also spurred by the fact that prices of imports are now relatively cheaper than prices at home. At the same time, the higher prices at home discourage exports abroad; the result is a deficit in the balance of payments, which must be paid for by foreign countries cashing in francs for gold. The gold outflow means that France must eventually contract its inflated paper francs in order to prevent a loss of all of its gold. If the inflation has taken the form of bank deposits, then the French banks have to contract their loans and deposits in order to avoid bankruptcy as foreigners call upon the French banks to redeem their deposits in gold. The contraction lowers prices at home, and generates an export surplus, thereby reversing the gold outflow, until the price levels are equalized in France and in other countries as well.

It is true that the interventions of governments previous to the nineteenth century weakened the speed of this market mechanism, and allowed for a business cycle of inflation and recession within this gold standard framework. These interventions were particularly: the governments' monopolizing of the mint, legal tender laws, the creation of paper money, and the development of inflationary banking propelled by each of the governments. But while these interventions slowed the adjustments of the market, these adjustments were still in ultimate control of the situation. So while the classical gold standard of the nineteenth century was not perfect, and allowed for relatively minor booms and busts, it still provided us with by far the best monetary order the world has ever known, an order which worked, which kept business cycles from getting out of hand, and which enabled the development of free international trade, exchange, and investment.[1]

2.
Phase II:
World War I and After

If the classical gold standard worked so well, why did it break down? It broke down because governments were entrusted with the task of keeping their monetary promises, of seeing to it that pounds, dollars, francs, etc., were always redeemable in gold as they and their controlled banking system had pledged. It was not gold that failed; it was the folly of trusting government to keep its promises. To wage the catastrophic war of World War I, each government had to inflate its own supply of paper and bank currency. So severe was this inflation that it was impossible for the warring governments to keep their pledges, and so they went "off the gold standard," i.e., declared their own bankruptcy, shortly after entering the war. All except the United States, which entered the war late, and did not inflate the supply of dollars enough to endanger redeemability. But, apart from the United States, the world suffered what some economists now hail as the

[1] For a recent study of the classical gold standard, and a history of the early phases of its breakdown in the twentieth century, see Melchior Palyi, *The Twilight of Gold,* 1914–1936 (Chicago: Henry Regnery, 1972).

Nirvana of freely-fluctuating exchange rates (now called "dirty floats"), competitive devaluations, warring currency blocs, exchange controls, tariffs and quotas, and the breakdown of international trade and investment. The inflated pounds, francs, marks, etc., depreciated in relation to gold and the dollar; monetary chaos abounded throughout the world.

In those days there were, happily, very few economists to hail this situation as the monetary ideal. It was generally recognized that Phase II was the threshold to international disaster, and politicians and economists looked around for ways to restore the stability and freedom of the classical gold standard.

3.
Phase III:
The Gold Exchange Standard (Britain and the United States) 1926–1931

How to return to the Golden Age? The sensible thing to do would have been to recognize the facts of reality, the fact of the depreciated pound, franc, mark, etc., and to return to the gold standard at a redefined rate: a rate that would recognize the existing supply of money and price levels. The British pound, for example, had been traditionally defined at a weight which made it equal to $4.86. But by the end of World War I, the inflation in Britain had brought the pound down to approximately $3.50 on the free foreign exchange market. Other currencies were similarly depreciated.

The sensible policy would have been for Britain to return to gold at approximately $3.50, and for the other inflated countries to do the same. Phase I could have been smoothly and rapidly restored. Instead, the British made the fateful decision to return to gold at the old par of $4.86.[2] It did so for reasons of British national "prestige," and in a vain attempt to reestablish London as the "hard money" financial center of the world. To succeed at this piece of heroic folly, Britain would have had to deflate severely its money supply and its price levels, for at a $4.86 pound British export prices were far too high to be competitive in the world markets. But deflation was now politically out of the question, for the growth of trade unions, buttressed by a nationwide system of unemployment insurance, had made wage rates rigid downward; in order to deflate, the British government would have had to reverse the growth of its welfare state. In fact, the British wished to continue to inflate money and prices. As a result of combining inflation with a return to an overvalued par, British exports were depressed all during the 1920s and unemployment was severe all during the period when most of the world was experiencing an economic boom.

How could the British try to have their cake and eat it at the same time? By establishing a new international monetary order which would induce or coerce *other* governments into inflating or into going back to gold at

[2] On the crucial British error and its consequence in leading to the 1929 depression, see Lionel Robbins, *The Great Depression* (New York: Macmillan, 1934).

overvalued pars for their own currencies, thus crippling their own exports and subsidizing imports from Britain. This is precisely what Britain did, as it led the way, at the Genoa Conference of 1922, in creating a new international monetary order, the gold-exchange standard.

The gold-exchange standard worked as follows: The United States remained on the classical gold standard, redeeming dollars in gold. Britain and the other countries of the West, however, returned to a pseudo-gold standard, Britain in 1926 and the other countries around the same time. British pounds and other currencies were not payable in gold coins, but only in large-sized bars, suitable only for international transactions. This prevented the ordinary citizens of Britain and other European countries from using gold in their daily life, and thus permitted a wider degree of paper and bank inflation. But furthermore, Britain redeemed pounds not merely in gold, but also in dollars; while the other countries redeemed their currencies not in gold, but in pounds. And most of these countries were induced by Britain to return to gold at overvalued parities. The result was a pyramiding of United States on gold, of British pounds on dollars, and of other European currencies on pounds—the "gold-exchange standard," with the dollar and the pound as the two "key currencies."

Now when Britain inflated, and experienced a deficit in its balance of payments, the gold standard mechanism did not work to quickly restrict British inflation. For instead of other countries redeeming their pounds for gold, they kept the pounds and inflated on top of them. Hence Britain and Europe were permitted to inflate unchecked, and British deficits could pile up unrestrained by the market discipline of the gold standard. As for the United States, Britain was able to induce the United States to inflate dollars so as not to lose many dollar reserves or gold to the United States.

The point of the gold-exchange standard is that it cannot last; the piper must eventually be paid, but only in a disastrous reaction to the lengthy inflationary boom. As sterling balances piled up in France, the United States, and elsewhere, the slightest loss of confidence in the increasingly shaky and jerry-built inflationary structure was bound to lead to general collapse. This is precisely what happened in 1931; the failure of inflated banks throughout Europe, and the attempt of "hard money" France to cash in its sterling balances for gold, led Britain to go off the gold standard completely. Britain was soon followed by the other countries of Europe.

4. Phase IV: Fluctuating Fiat Currencies, 1931–1945

The world was now back to the monetary chaos of World War I, except that now there seemed to be little hope for a restoration of gold. The international economic order had disintegrated into the chaos of clean and dirty floating exchange rates, competing devaluations, exchange controls, and trade barriers;

international economic and monetary warfare raged between currencies and currency blocs. International trade and investment came to a virtual standstill; and trade was conducted through barter agreements conducted by governments competing and conflicting with one another. Secretary of State Cordell Hull repeatedly pointed out that these monetary and economic conflicts of the 1930s were the major cause of World War II.[3]

The United States remained on the gold standard for two years, and then, in 1933–34, went off the classical gold standard in a vain attempt to get out of the depression. American citizens could no longer redeem dollars in gold, and were even prohibited from owning any gold, either here or abroad. But the United States remained, after 1934, on a peculiar new form of gold standard, in which the dollar, now redefined to 1/35 of a gold ounce, was redeemable in gold to foreign governments and Central Banks. A lingering tie to gold remained. Furthermore, the monetary chaos in Europe led to gold flowing into the only relatively safe monetary haven, the United States.

The chaos and the unbridled economic warfare of the 1930s points up an important lesson: the grievous *political* flaw (apart from the economic problems) in the Milton Friedman-Chicago School monetary scheme for freely-fluctuating fiat currencies. For what the Friedmanites would do—*in the name of the free*

---

[3] Cordell Hull, *Memoirs* (New York, 1948), vol. I, p. 81. Also see Richard N. Gardner, *Sterling-Dollar Conspiracy* (Oxford: Clarendon Press, 1956), p. 141.

market—is to cut all ties to gold completely, leave the absolute control of each national currency in the hands of its central government issuing fiat paper as legal tender—*and then* advise each government to allow its currency to fluctuate freely with respect to all other fiat currencies, as well as to refrain from inflating its currency too outrageously. The grave political flaw is to hand total control of the money supply to the Nation-State, and then to hope and expect that the State will refrain from using that power. And since power always tends to be used, including the power to counterfeit legally, the naivete, as well as the statist nature, of this type of program should be starkly evident.

And so, the disastrous experience of Phase IV, the 1930s world of fiat paper and economic warfare, led the United States authorities to adopt as their major economic war aim of World War II the restoration of a viable international monetary order, an order on which could be built a renaissance of world trade and the fruits of the international division of labor.

5. Phase V: Bretton Woods and the New Gold Exchange Standard (the United States) 1945–1968

The new international monetary order was conceived and then driven through by the United States at an international monetary conference at Bretton

Woods, New Hampshire, in mid-1944, and ratified by the Congress in July, 1945. While the Bretton Woods system worked far better than the disaster of the 1930s, it worked only as another inflationary recrudescence of the gold-exchange standard of the 1920s and—like the 1920s—the system lived only on borrowed time.

The new system was essentially the gold-exchange standard of the 1920s but with the dollar rudely displacing the British pound as one of the "key currencies." Now the dollar, valued at 1/35 of a gold ounce, was to be the *only* key currency. The other difference from the 1920s was that the dollar was no longer redeemable in gold to American citizens; instead, the 1930's system was continued, with the dollar redeemable in gold *only* to foreign governments and their Central Banks. No private individuals, only governments, were to be allowed the privilege of redeeming dollars in the world gold currency. In the Bretton Woods system, the United States pyramided dollars (in paper money and in bank deposits) on top of gold, in which dollars could be redeemed by foreign governments; while all other governments held dollars as their basic reserve and pyramided their currency on top of dollars. And since the United States began the post-war world with a huge stock of gold (approximately $25 billion) there was plenty of play for pyramiding dollar claims on top of it. Furthermore, the system could "work" for a while because all the world's currencies returned to the new system at their pre-World War II pars, most of which were highly overvalued in terms of their inflated and depreciated currencies. The inflated pound sterling, for example, returned at $4.86, even though it was worth far less than that in terms of purchasing power on the market. Since the dollar was artificially undervalued and most other currencies overvalued in 1945, the dollar was made scarce, and the world suffered from a so-called dollar shortage, which the American taxpayer was supposed to be obligated to make up by foreign aid. In short, the export surplus enjoyed by the undervalued American dollar was to be partly financed by the hapless American taxpayer in the form of foreign aid.

There being plenty of room for inflation before retribution could set in, the United States government embarked on its post-war policy of continual monetary inflation, a policy it has pursued merrily ever since. By the early 1950s, the continuing American inflation began to turn the tide of international trade. For while the United States was inflating and expanding money and credit, the major European governments, many of them influenced by "Austrian" monetary advisers, pursued a relatively "hard money" policy (e.g., West Germany, Switzerland, France, Italy). Steeply inflationist Britain was compelled by its outflow of dollars to devalue the pound to more realistic levels (for a while it was approximately $2.40). All this, combined with the increasing productivity of Europe, and later Japan, led to continuing balance of payments deficits with the United States. As the 1950s and 1960s wore on, the United States became more and more inflationist, both absolutely and relatively to Japan and Western Europe. But the classical gold standard check on inflation—especially American inflation—was gone. For the rules of the Bretton Woods game provided that the West European countries had to keep piling up their reserve, and even use these dollars as a base to inflate their own currency and credit.

But as the 1950s and 1960s continued, the harder-money countries of West Europe (and Japan) became restless at being forced to pile up dollars that were now increasingly overvalued instead of undervalued. As the purchasing power and hence the true value of dollars fell, they became increasingly unwanted by foreign governments. But they were locked into a system that was more and more of a nightmare. The American reaction to the European complaints, headed by France and DeGaulle's major monetary adviser, the classical gold-standard economist Jacques Rueff, was merely scorn and brusque dismissal. American politicians and economists simply declared that Europe was *forced* to use the dollar as its currency, that it could do nothing about its growing problems, and therefore the United States could keep blithely inflating while pursuing a policy of "benign neglect" toward the international monetary consequences of its own actions.

But Europe did have the legal option of redeeming dollars in gold at $35 an ounce. And as the dollar became increasingly overvalued in terms of hard money currencies and gold, European governments began more and more to exercise that option. The gold standard check was coming into use; hence gold flowed steadily out of the United States for two decades after the early

1950s, until the United States gold stock dwindled over this period from over $20 billion to $9 billion. As dollars kept inflating upon a dwindling gold base, how could the United States keep redeeming foreign dollars in gold—the cornerstone of the Bretton Woods system? These problems did not slow down continued United States inflation of dollars and prices, or the United States policy of "benign neglect," which resulted by the late 1960s in an accelerated pileup of no less than $80 billion in unwanted dollars in Europe (known as Eurodollars). To try to stop European redemption of dollars into gold, the United States exerted intense political pressure on the European governments, similar but on a far larger scale to the British cajoling of France not to redeem its heavy sterling balances until 1931. But economic law has a way, at long last, of catching up with governments, and this is what happened to the inflation-happy United States government by the end of the 1960s. The gold-exchange system of Bretton Woods—hailed by the United States political and economic Establishment as permanent and impregnable—began to unravel rapidly in 1968.

6.
Phase VI:
The Unraveling of Bretton Woods, 1968–1971

As dollars piled up abroad and gold continued to flow outward, the United States found it increasingly difficult to maintain the price of gold at $35 an ounce in the free gold markets at London and Zurich. Thirty-five dollars an ounce was the keystone of the system, and while American citizens have been barred since 1934 from owning gold anywhere in the world, other citizens have enjoyed the freedom to own gold bullion and coin. Hence, one way for individual Europeans to redeem their dollars in gold was to sell their dollars for gold at $35 an ounce in the free gold market. As the dollar kept inflating and depreciating, and as American balance of payments deficits continued, Europeans and other private citizens began to accelerate their sales of dollars into gold. In order to keep the dollar at $35 an ounce, the United States government was forced to leak out gold from its dwindling stock to support the $35 price at London and Zurich.

A crisis of confidence in the dollar on the free gold markets led the United States to effect a fundamental change in the monetary system in March 1968. The idea was to stop the pesky free gold market from ever again endangering the Bretton Woods arrangement. Hence was born the "two-tier gold market." The idea was that the free gold market could go to blazes; it would be strictly insulated from the *real* monetary action in the Central Banks and governments of the world. The United States would no longer try to keep the free-market gold price at $35; it would ignore the free gold market, and it and all the other governments agreed to keep the value of the dollar at $35 an ounce forevermore. The governments and

Central Banks of the world would henceforth buy no more gold from the "outside" market and would sell no more gold to that market; from now on gold would simply move as counters from one Central Bank to another, and new gold supplies, free gold market, or private demand for gold would take their own course completely separated from the monetary arrangements of the world.

Along with this, the United States pushed hard for the new launching of a new kind of world paper reserve, Special Drawing Rights (SDRs), which it was hoped would eventually replace gold altogether and serve as a new world paper currency to be issued by a future World Reserve Bank; if such a system were ever established, then the United States could inflate unchecked forevermore, in collaboration with other world governments (the only limit would then be the disastrous one of a worldwide runaway inflation and the crackup of the world paper currency). But the SDRs, combatted intensely as they have been by Western Europe and the "hard-money" countries, have so far been only a small supplement to American and other currency reserves.

All pro-paper economists, from Keynesians to Friedmanites, were now confident that gold would disappear from the international monetary system; cut off from its "support" by the dollar, these economists all confidently predicted, the free-market gold price would soon fall below $35 an ounce, and even down to the estimated "industrial" nonmonetary gold price of $10 an ounce. Instead, the free price of gold, never below $35, had been steadily above $35, and by early 1973 had climbed to around $125 an ounce, a figure that no pro-paper economist would have thought possible as recently as a year earlier.

Far from establishing a permanent new monetary system, the two-tier gold market only bought a few years of time; American inflation and deficits continued. Eurodollars accumulated rapidly, gold continued to flow outward, and the higher free-market price of gold simply revealed the accelerated loss of world confidence in the dollar. The two-tier system moved rapidly toward crisis—and to the final dissolution of Bretton Woods.[4]

7.
Phase VII:
The End of Bretton Woods:
Fluctuating Fiat Currencies,
August–December 1971

On August 15, 1971, at the same time that President Nixon imposed a price-wage freeze in a vain attempt to check bounding inflation, Mr. Nixon also brought the postwar Bretton Woods system to a crashing end. As European Central Banks at last threatened to redeem much of their swollen stock of

[4] On the two-tier gold market, see Jacques Rueff, *The Monetary Sin of the West* (New York: Macmillan, 1972).

dollars for gold, President Nixon went totally off gold. For the first time in American history, the dollar was totally fiat, totally without backing in gold. Even the tenuous link with gold maintained since 1933 was now severed. The world was plunged into the fiat system of the thirties—and worse, since now even the dollar was no longer linked to gold. Ahead loomed the dread spectre of currency blocs, competing devaluations, economic warfare, and the breakdown of international trade and investment, with the worldwide depression that would then ensue.

What to do? Attempting to restore an international monetary order lacking a link to gold, the United States led the world into the Smithsonian Agreement on December 18, 1971.

8.
Phase VIII: The Smithsonian Agreement, December 1971–February 1973

The Smithsonian Agreement, hailed by President Nixon as the "greatest monetary agreement in the history of the world," was even more shaky and unsound than the gold-exchange standard of the 1920s or than Bretton Woods. For once again, the countries of the world pledged to maintain fixed exchange rates, but this time with no gold or world money to give any currency backing. Furthermore, many European currencies were fixed at undervalued parities in relation to the dollar; the only United States concession was a puny devaluation of the official dollar rate to $38 an ounce. But while much too little and too late, this devaluation was significant in violating an endless round of official American pronouncements, which had pledged to maintain the $35 rate forevermore. Now at last the $35 price was implicitly acknowledged as not graven on tablets of stone.

It was inevitable that fixed exchange rates, even with wider agreed zones of fluctuation, but lacking a world medium of exchange, were doomed to rapid defeat. This was especially true since American inflation of money and prices, the decline of the dollar, and balance of payments deficits continued unchecked.

The swollen supply of Eurodollars, combined with the continued inflation and the removal of gold backing, drove the free-market gold price up to $215 an ounce. And as the overvaluation of the dollar and the undervaluation of European and Japanese hard money became increasingly evident, the dollar finally broke apart on the world markets in the panic months of February–March 1973. It became impossible for West Germany, Switzerland, France and the other hard money countries to continue to buy dollars in order to support the dollar at an overvalued rate. In little over a year, the Smithsonian system of fixed exchange rates without gold had smashed apart on the rocks of economic reality.

9.
Phase IX: Fluctuating Fiat Currencies, March 1973–?

With the dollar breaking apart, the world shifted again, to a system of fluctuating fiat currencies. Within the West European bloc, exchange rates were tied to one another, and the United States again devalued the official dollar rate by a token amount to $42 an ounce. As the dollar plunged in foreign exchange from day to day, and the West German mark, the Swiss franc, and the Japanese yen hurtled upward, the American authorities, backed by the Friedmanite economists, began to think that this was the monetary ideal. It is true that dollar surpluses and sudden balance of payments crises do not plague the world under fluctuating exchange rates. Furthermore, American export firms began to chortle that falling dollar rates made American goods cheaper abroad, and therefore benefitted exports. It is true that governments persisted in interfering with exchange fluctuations ("dirty" instead of "clean" floats), but overall it seemed that the international monetary order had sundered into a Friedmanite utopia.

But it became clear all too soon that all is far from well in the current international monetary system. The long-run problem is that the hard-money countries will not sit by forever and watch their currencies become more expensive and their exports hurt for the benefit of their American competitors. If American inflation and dollar depreciation continues, they will soon shift to the competing devaluation, exchange controls, currency blocs, and economic warfare of the 1930s. But more immediate is the other side of the coin: the fact that depreciating dollars means that American imports are far more expensive, American tourists suffer abroad, and cheap exports are snapped up by foreign countries so rapidly as to raise prices of exports at home (e.g., the American wheat-and-meat price inflation). So that American exporters might indeed benefit, but only at the expense of the inflation-ridden American consumer. The crippling uncertainty of rapid exchange rate fluctuations was brought starkly home to Americans with the rapid plunge of the dollar in foreign exchange markets in July 1973.

Since the United States went completely off gold in August 1971 and established the Friedmanite fluctuating fiat system in March 1973, the United States and the world have suffered the most intense and most sustained bout of peacetime inflation in the history of the world. It should be clear by now that this is scarcely a coincidence. Before the dollar was cut loose from gold, Keynesians and Friedmanites, each in their own way devoted to fiat paper money, confidently predicted that when fiat money was established, the market price of gold would fall promptly to its nonmonetary level, then estimated at about $8 an ounce. In their scorn of gold, both groups maintained that it was the mighty dollar that was propping up the price of gold, and not vice versa. Since 1971, the market price of gold has never been below the old fixed price of $35 an ounce, and has almost always been enormously higher. When, during the 1950s and 1960s, economists such as Jacques Rueff were calling for a gold standard at a price of $70 an ounce, the price was considered absurdly high. It is now even more absurdly low. The far higher gold price is an indication of the calamitous deterioration of the dollar since "modern" economists had their way and all gold backing was removed.

It is now all too clear that the world has become fed up with the unprecedented inflation, in the United States and throughout the world, that has been sparked by the fluctuating fiat currency era inaugurated in 1973. We are also weary of the extreme volatility and unpredictability of currency exchange rates. This volatility is the consequence of the national fiat money system, which fragmented the world's money and added artificial political instability to the natural uncertainty in the free-market price system. The Friedmanite dream of fluctuating fiat money lies in ashes, and there is an understandable yearning to return to an international money with fixed exchange rates.

Unfortunately, the classical gold standard lies forgotten, and the ultimate goal of most American and world leaders is the old Keynesian vision of a one-world fiat paper standard, a new currency unit issued by a World Reserve Bank (WRB). Whether the new currency be termed "the bancor" (offered by Keynes), the "unita" (proposed by World War II United States Treasury official Harry Dexter White), or the "phoenix" (suggested by *The Economist*) is unimportant. The vital point is that such an international paper currency, while indeed free of balance of payments crises since the WRB could issue as much bancors as it wished and supply them to its country of choice, would provide for an open channel for unlimited world-wide inflation, unchecked by either balance-of-payments crises or by declines in exchange rates. The WRB would then be the all-powerful determinant of the world's money supply and its national distribution. The WRB could and would subject the world to what it believes will be a wisely-controlled inflation. Unfortunately, there would then be nothing standing in the way of the unimaginably catastrophic economic holocaust of world-wide runaway inflation, nothing, that is, except the dubious capacity of the WRB to fine-tune the world economy.

While a world-wide paper unit and Central Bank remain the ultimate goal of world's Keynesian-oriented leaders, the more realistic and proximate goal is a return to a glorified Bretton Woods scheme, except this time without the check of any backing in gold. Already the world's major Central Banks are attempting to "coordinate" monetary and economic policies, harmonize rates of inflation, and fix exchange rates. The militant drive for a European paper currency issued by a European Central Bank seems on the verge of success. This goal is being sold to the gullible public by the fallacious claim that a free-trade European Economic Community (EEC) necessarily requires an overarching European bureaucracy, a uniformity of taxation throughout the EEC, and, in particular, a European Central Bank and paper unit. Once that is achieved, closer coordination with the Federal Reserve and other major Central Banks will follow immediately. And then, could a World Central Bank be far behind? Short of that ultimate goal, however, we may soon be plunged into yet another Bretton Woods, with all the attendant crises of the balance of payments and Gresham's Law that follow from fixed exchange rates in a world of fiat moneys.

As we face the future, the prognosis for the dollar and for the international monetary system is grim indeed. Until and unless we return to the classical gold standard at a realistic gold price, the international money system is fated to shift back and forth between fixed and fluctuating exchange rates with each system posing unsolved problems, working badly, and finally disintegrating. And fueling this disintegration will be the continued inflation of the supply of dollars and hence of American prices which show no sign of abating. The prospect for the future is accelerating and eventually runaway inflation at home, accompanied by monetary breakdown and economic warfare abroad. This prognosis can only be changed by a drastic alteration of the American and world monetary system: by the return to a free market commodity money such as gold, and by removing government totally from the monetary scene.

Index

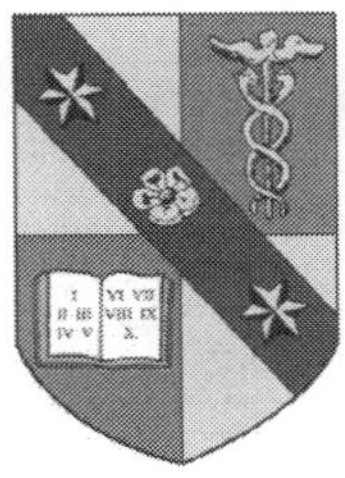

About the Mises Institute

The Ludwig von Mises Institute was founded in 1982 as the research and educational center of classical liberalism, libertarian political theory, and the Austrian School of economics.

It serves as the world's leading provider of educational materials, conferences, media, and literature in support of the tradition of thought represented by Ludwig von Mises and the school of thought he enlivened and carried forward during the twentieth century, which has now blossomed into a massive international movement of students, professors, professionals, and people in all walks of life.

It seeks a radical shift in the intellectual climate as the foundation for a renewal of the free and prosperous commonwealth. It is the mission of the Mises Institute to place human choice at the center of economic theory, to encourage a revival of critical historical research, and to advance the Misesian tradition of thought through the defense of the market economy, private property, sound money, and peaceful international relations, while opposing government intervention as economically and socially destructive.

The Mises Institute has 350-plus faculty members working with it on one or more academic projects. With their help, and thousands of donors in 50 states and 80 foreign countries, the Institute has held more than 1,000 teaching conferences, including the Mises University, and seminars on subjects from monetary policy to the history of war, as well as international and interdisciplinary Austrian Scholars Conferences.

You can visit us at Mises.org. You can subscribe to our services. You will find an extensive book catalog that includes this title, with discounts on volume purchases.

We welcome your support of our work.

Made in the USA
Middletown, DE
17 October 2023